Beautiful Dolls Made Easy

The Complete Book on Porcelain Dollmaking

by Helen Schaeffer

Photographs by Lilly Smith

Published by Scott Publications
30595 Eight Mile
Livonia, MI 48152-1798

Printed in U.S.A.
First Printing 1994
Second Printing 1997

ISBN 0-916-809-92-7
Library of Congress Catalog Card Number 97-66094

Table of Contents

Dedication

. . . to my family, who good-naturedly puts up with my doll things everywhere; and especially to Stan, my husband and best friend, who encourages and supports me, and tries his best to understand my "doll passion" . . .

I dedicate this book with love.

Helen Schaeffer

Introduction

PORCELAIN DOLLMAKING, whether the replication of contemporary or antique dolls, is both a many-faceted craft and an art. Today's dollmaker draws on dollmaking history while combining the skills of a high-fire ceramist with the artistry of a china painter, the eye of a fashion designer, and the expertise and nimble fingers of a wigmaker, seamstress, and shoemaker to create the heirlooms of the future. The Golden Age of Dollmaking (1880s to 1920s) produced dolls of incredible beauty and character. These wonderful creations have served to inspire a new generation of dollmakers who, with today's technology and know-how, are producing dolls of unsurpassed beauty and perfection.

When I began my porcelain dollmaking adventure twenty plus years ago, there were no concise written directions. Supplies were meager or nonexistent, and much of what we take for granted today had not yet been thought of. Many valuable and sometimes expensive lessons were learned from the process of trial and error.

The primary purpose of this book is to save the reader that "trial and error" experience. I wanted to give you what I would have welcomed so long ago: a complete reference book to both guide the novice, step-by-step, through the intricacies of dollmaking and supply the more seasoned dollmaker with solutions for specific problems.

Additionally, it is my fervent desire to open the reader's mind to the wonders and possibilities of porcelain dollmaking. Dollmaking can be a most rewarding hobby, a method of producing memorable gifts, and has the potential to provide a successful venture into the world of business. The well-executed porcelain doll is a valuable commodity and is destined to become the collectible and antique of the future.

1 Where Did It Begin?

SHROUDED IN MYSTERY, perhaps no other substance in the world has had the fascinating history of porcelain. The first true porcelain was made in China around 850 A.D. during the T'ang dynasty, when the newly-discovered petuntse (a feldspathic rock) was added to china clay (kaolin) and fired, resulting in a vitreous, partially translucent clay body. The Chinese rigorously guarded the secret of their porcelain formula and kept that secret within the family structure.

One of the largest of the Tête Jumeaux is this beautiful number *15* made by Maison Jumeau, France, around 1890.

Marco Polo, while working in the service of the Khublai Khan (1275-1292), is believed to be the first European to see Chinese porcelain, and Polo is credited with giving porcelain its name. He called it *porcellana,* the Italian name for cowrie shells. When Polo returned to Venice, he undoubtedly brought along some pieces of this wondrous new substance. These "treasures" and pieces brought by later travelers to the Far East created quite a stir and set off a frantic rush among European nobility to acquire more of this precious commodity.

During the Middle Ages, small quantities of prized porcelains found their way to the courts of Europe via brave entrepreneurs, who risked highwaymen, piracy, shipwrecks, and warfare to bring these wares to Europe. Porcelain was accorded an esteem usually reserved for jewels and precious metals, and the porcelains that did reach Europe were so treasured that they were often encased in jewel-encrusted gold and silver mounts for protection. European nobility jealously coveted and craved more porcelains. The solution was, of course, to manufacture this beautiful ware on the continent; but try as they might, the secret of Chinese porcelain eluded them.

The first recorded attempt at the duplication of Chinese porcelain was the soft paste Medici porcelain made in Florence around 1575. This grayish-glazed, often-misshapened ware wasn't considered an acceptable alternative to Chinese porcelain, and Europeans continued to import this prized ware from the Orient.

In 1602, the Dutch formed the Dutch East India Company, and reliable trade with the Far East soon ensued. Between 1602 and 1657, historians estimate over 3,000,000 pieces of Chinese porcelain were brought to Europe on Dutch ships.

Over a century after the Medici porcelain attempt, Augustus II "The Strong," brought together Count von Tschirnhaus, a nobleman interested in the scientific process of making porcelain, with Johann Friedrich Böttger, an alchemist who had led Augustus to believe that he could turn lead into gold. Böttger, of course, failed at his attempts to produce gold, but records show that on January 15, 1708, without prior knowledge of porcelain production, he succeeded in producing a material very similar to Chinese porcelain and equal in hardness, translucency, and quality. Augustus, who already owned one of the most extensive porcelain collections in all of Europe, was delighted with Böttger's discovery, and in 1710, he directed that the Royal Saxon Porcelain Manufactory be established in Meissen.

Unlike the Chinese, the Europeans could not keep the porcelain formula a secret, and rivals proliferated from Vienna through the Rhineland to Italy, France, Spain, Denmark, Russia, Switzerland, and England. The production of porcelain became big business in Germany, and so it was only natural that in Germany, with an abundance of raw materials plus forests of trees to supply fuel, skilled craftsmen would begin to use this beautiful material to produce doll heads.

Doll heads made of china were produced in Germany as early as the 1750s. These china head dolls were costly and available only to the aristocracy until commercial production began in the 1840s. Most early china heads were unmarked; however, some do bear the mark of Meissen, Königliche Porzellanmanufaktur (K.P.M.), and Royal Copenhagen.

By the 1860s, the china head doll was being replaced in popularity by the bisque doll because bisque (unglazed porcelain) had a more natural appearance. Early bisque dolls were lady dolls known as French Fashion dolls or *parisiennes,* and most were French made by firms such as Gaultier, Jumeau, Bru, Mme. Rohmer, Gesland, and Huret. It is very likely that heads for some French dolls were indeed produced in Germany. French fashion lady dolls had not only beautiful faces, but were elaborately clothed, coiffed, and ornamented to reflect the very latest in the fashion world. These magnificent dolls were a luxury even in their day, costing anywhere from five to over one hundred dollars. At the same time, German firms such as J. D. Kestner, Kling & Co., and Alt, Beck & Gottschalck of the Waltershausen/Ohrdruf area were busy turning out German bisque heads. These early heads were the lady-type dolls of untinted bisque with molded hair called Parians; but in no time, the Germans were copying the French fashion dolls.

Glazed porcelain head, typical for a simple style china doll. Made circa 1860 in Germany, she is referred to as a "flat-top china" with the black hair parted in center and curls around the head.

The German doll industry proliferated throughout Thüringia, an area already known for its toy production. The towns of Waltershausen and Sonneberg were particularly synonymous with dolls. In spite of the size of the German dollmaking industry, there were few factories that produced all the components for an entire doll. Rather, the Germans made ingenious use of home industry. Entire families, parents, grandparents, and children worked side by side in their homes, each producing some facet of the complete doll. Families specialized; there were families of pressers who made the bodies; glass blowers, shoe makers, and wig makers. The German "cottage industry" enabled the German doll manufacturers to produce a good doll at a cheap price and thus compete with the French doll industry.

In 1878, Emile Jumeau introduced a new type of doll. The *bébé,* with its childlike body, quickly replaced the fashion lady in popularity. These dolls, modeled after pampered French children of the period, were soon made by various other French firms such as Bru, François Gaultier, Jules Nicolas Steiner, Schmitt & Fils, Rabery & Delphieu, and A. Thuillier.

Glass-eyed *K★R-114 Gretchen* by Kämmer & Reinhardt, Germany, is the rare version of the character doll, sculpted with Mr. Reinhardt's grandson as the model in 1910. Comes also with painted eyes (more common) and as a boy doll, *Hans.*

German manufacturers countered with the German child doll, often referred to as the "dolly-face" doll. The Germans offered such innovations as sleep eyes, flirty eyes, open mouths with teeth, voice and walking mechanisms, real eyelashes and eyebrows, and other novelties. Large German manufacturers of these sweet faces included the factories of J. D. Kestner, Simon & Halbig, Armand Marseille, and Kämmer & Reinhardt.

By the end of the century, the German doll manufacturers were supplying two-thirds of the world's dolls. In spite of her beauty, the French doll simply could not compete with her less-expensive, well-made German sister. The S. F. B. J. (Société Française de Fabrication de Bébés et Jouets), founded in 1899, was a coalition of several prominent French dollmakers and one German importer of toys and dolls. This consortium hoped that by this merger, they could produce a less-expensive doll and so

In simple frock or elaborate costume, the Long-face Jumeau (*Jumeau Triste*) is one of the most sought-after bébés. She was made circa 1878-1890 by Maison Jumeau, France, and is marked with only a number.

become more competitive with the German doll industry.

With a new century came yet another innovation in dollmaking. The early 1900s was a time of enormous social change. German doll designers responded to the new era by introducing the Character doll. The public was tiring of the dolly-face doll. They responded positively to these new, simply-dressed, realistic portraits of children. Starting in 1909, Kämmer & Reinhardt introduced a number of these lovely, real-looking dolls, including the beloved mold *101* (*Peter and Marie*). Other German companies including Bähr & Pröschild; Hertel, Schwab & Co.; Simon & Halbig; Gebrüder Heubach; J.D. Kestner; and Armand Marseille quickly jumped aboard the bandwagon. By 1911, the French S.F.B.J. advertised character dolls and introduced such unforgettable faces as the *252 Pouty* and the so-called smiling or laughing Jumeau.

Interrupted briefly by World War I, the German dollmaking industry flourished through the early part of the century until the 1930s. The French S.F.B.J. continued to manufacture dolls during the war and reportedly produced dolls through the 1950s.

Porcelain dollmaking never made it as an industry in the United States. There were some early pottery dolls made in Virginia, and the Fulper Pottery Co. of Flemington, N.J., produced a line of mediocre porcelain dolls from 1918 to 1921. However, it is in America that the present-day reproduction dollmaking hobby industry has its roots.

Elaborately costumed French Fashion doll *Stobé* in the "portrait" range of Jumeau with antique trunk and accessories.

MILDRED AND VERNON SEELEY of Oneonta, New York, founded Seeley's Ceramic Service in 1946. Mildred's love of antique dolls soon led her to introduce dollmaking as a hobby, and Seeley's began supplying the needs of the porcelain dollmaking hobbyist. When the Seeleys retired in 1977, the company was purchased by Rolf and Ragnhild Ericson, who quickly recognized the need for dollmaking education. Almost immediately, the Doll Artisan Guild was founded. Today the Guild, with thousands of members, is recognized not only as being the world's largest organization of dollmakers but for its excellent magazine, *The Doll Artisan,* and for its prestigious Doll Artisan Guild School of Dollmaking. The Doll Artisan Guild has become synonymous with excellence in dollmaking.

All major innovation in the present-day porcelain dollmaking industry came about through the Seeley organization. Outstanding molds, the best porcelain slip available today, the waterbase china-painting technique, new media, the Dust-free Cleaning Technique, worksheets and books, quality composition bodies, and specialty brushes have all been introduced or improved by Seeley's to give today's dollmaker the advantage of working with the very best. The company continues to research and develop better products and introduces new and exciting techniques throughout the world.

Today the Doll Artisan Guild School of Dollmaking offers an educational program that is unrivaled throughout the world. The Apprentice Program takes the beginning dollmaker, step by step, through the entire dollmaking process of casting molds, dust-free greenware cleaning, waterbase china-painting technique, and stringing and completing dolls.

The student progresses from simple baby dolls, through more difficult German dolls, culminating with French dolls, all under the expert guidance of Doll Artisan Guild (D.A.G.) Instructors. Completion of the three Apprentice courses leads to becoming a Certified Doll Artisan. From there, the student can continue his or her quest for knowledge with specialty seminars such as Mechanical Dolls, French Fashion Dolls, Parians, Clowns, Modern Dolls, and many more. One can become a certified Seeley Doll Products Teacher and go on to earn the titles of D.A.G. Master of Dollmaking, D.A.G. Grand Master of Dollmaking, and D.A.G. Doctor of Dollmaking.

Most recently, the Guild has introduced yet another milestone in dollmaking - the Credit Recommendation Program (CRP). This new program allows the student to earn a credit recommendation of three semester hours toward a college degree.

Each year, the Doll Artisan Guild hosts International Doll Conventions throughout the world to bring dollmakers together to share their knowledge, learn even more about the fascinating hobby of dollmaking, and enter the renowned D.A.G. competitions.

I can think of no other organization in the world that gives one so much for so little; and therefore, if you love dolls and dollmaking, I highly recommend that you join the Doll Artisan Guild today and become a part of modern-day dollmaking history.

J.D. Kestner's solemn-looking child doll from the early 1890s, marked *#169*, can here be seen (left) together with the character child, *K★R-101 Marie*, circa 1910, and the somewhat later character baby, *K★R-121*, both by Kämmer & Reinhardt, Germany.

The Bru Jeune Bébés from the 1880s are considered the most exquisite of all bébés from the Bru factory, then under the leadership of Henri Chevrot.

Photos in Chapter 1 by Ragnhild Ericson

2 Mold Selection and Care

THERE ARE SO MANY MOLDS available to the dollmaker today that you may wonder where to start. My recommendation would be to select a mold for a doll that you really love and begin with a simple two-piece mold from a reputable manufacturer. Seeley molds (which were used for the projects in this book) are made of a high-quality, dense potter's plaster and have the properties of rapid water absorption, good release time, and excellent strength. These characteristics make molds easy to pour, capable of producing excellent detailed greenware, and long wearing. Molds can be quite an investment; but with proper care, quality molds will serve you well through many pourings.

How exactly do molds perform their job? When porcelain slip is poured into a mold, the water is drawn out of the slip and absorbed by the plaster walls of the mold, leaving a build-up of clay against the walls of the mold. When this clay build-up has reached the desired thickness, the remaining porcelain slip is drained from the mold, leaving the casting along the sides of the mold. The plaster of the mold continues to absorb water from the casting so that it becomes what we refer to as leatherhard (the stage at which the still-wet casting can be safely removed from the mold and retain its shape when handled).

Plaster molds will continue to absorb water during repeated pourings until they become saturated. Wet molds cannot do the job that they were intended to do. Keep this point in mind if your new mold arrives wet. Place the banded mold on several thicknesses of newspaper in a well-ventilated area and allow it to dry naturally. Rotate the mold and change the newspapers, as the paper absorbs the moisture from the mold. Never, never force dry a mold by placing it in the oven, microwave, or kiln. Heat will cause the plaster to deteriorate and shorten the life of your mold.

Before pouring your new mold, open it up to inspect it for any damage or debris. The mold should open easily. If the mold will not open, do not force it. Never attempt to pry two parts of a mold apart. To do so will chip the plaster and possibly break off the mold keys. If a mold does not open easily, run a little warm water over the seam lines. Wait about five minutes and try opening it again. Often a firm thump on the seam of the mold using the heal of your hand will cause the mold to open. If a mold continues to resist opening, fill the mold with warm water and drain it immediately. Wait another five minutes and open.

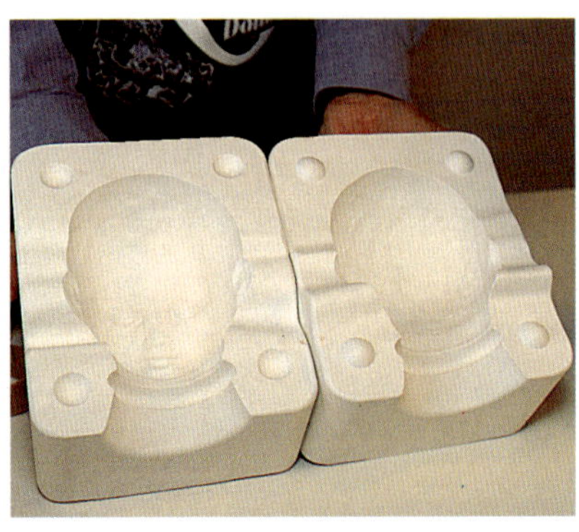

New molds may come to you held together with rubber bands or with plastic straps which need to be cut off and replaced with rubber bands. Molds must always be securely banded together with at least two rubber bands. Nylon banding straps are available in several lengths and are recommended for use when pouring large molds. It is very trau-

Mark the face part of the head mold with a china marker.

matic to have porcelain leak out of a mold and all over you and the floor because of inadequate banding! Be cautious - use an extra band or two.

Molds should be clearly marked and stored on sturdy shelves with the pourhole down or covered to keep out dirt, insects, and other creatures. Use a china marking pencil (from your local office supply store) to identify molds. It is also advisable to mark the face of a head mold so that you will know which half of the mold to take off first when removing a casting. China markers come in all colors; so to keep your molds organized and easy to locate, you could use one color for baby dolls, another color for all-bisque dolls, yet another for French dolls, and so on.

Before and after using a mold, always blow it out or use a soft brush to gently clean the inside of the mold. Every time a mold is used, all slip and clay particles should be removed from the pourhole and outside of the mold with a plastic mold cleaning knife, nylon mold scraper, or nylon fettling knife. Never clean the mold with anything sharp that might damage the plaster. When molds are not in use, be sure to keep mold halves firmly banded together. Molds allowed to dry open and/or unbanded may warp.

A frequently-asked question about pouring is, "How often can I pour the mold?" One should not attempt to pour more than two or three castings in one day. More frequent consecutive pours will result in the mold becoming too wet, and this saturation will cause the plaster to deteriorate. After three pours, allow the mold to rest and dry for a day or two. The size of the mold, temperature, and humidity will all influence the number of times you can pour the mold in a day. If you need to pour a large number of an item in a short period of time, you would do well to purchase an additional mold or two.

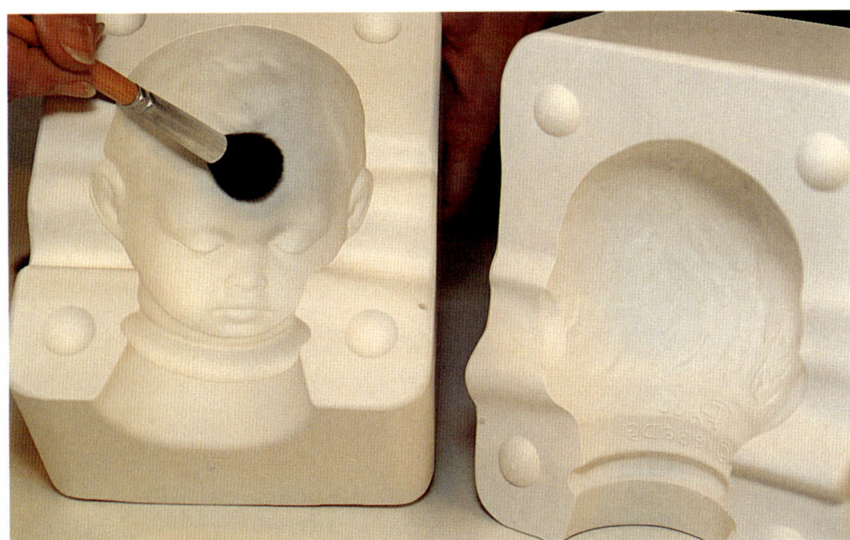
Before and after using a mold, use a soft brush to gently clean the inside of the mold.

Molds that are overpoured and not allowed to dry between pourings will often develop white fur-like crystals over the outside surface of the mold. This growth occurs as the deflocculant in the slip leaches through the wet plaster of the mold. The crystals can simply be brushed off, but their very presence is telling you to slow down and allow your molds time to dry out between pourings.

Occasionally, you may have a very dry mold on the shelf. Molds that are bone dry will not absorb the water from the slip evenly; therefore, it is wise to use a spray bottle to lightly mist the inside of the mold with a little water.

Sooner or later, you will encounter a mold that breaks or chips due to improper opening or handling or just overuse. While you are better off throwing out a mold that falls and breaks into a number of pieces, a broken key or other small piece of plaster (especially if it is not on the face) is another matter. Gently clean the mold surface with denatured alcohol, allow it to dry, and glue the pieces back together using a white craft glue such as *Elmer's* or *Tacky*. Greenware cast from such a repaired mold will require a little more attention when cleaning, but this is sometimes a worthwhile consideration in light of the expense of purchasing a new mold.

Preparing a Workplace

Dolls and dollmaking have a tendency to take over the house; from kitchen counters, to dining room table, to laundry room sink, to the bedroom floor . . . dolly things accumulate everywhere. This is the voice of experience speaking. My family can tell you that in spite of having had her own doll studio, "mother's doll thing" took over the entire house!

Wouldn't it be nice to have a room just for dollmaking activities? So much time could be saved if work-in-progress could be left out, readily accessible perchance some precious free time appears in our hectic daily schedule. Luckily for me, I live in a big, old house with room to spare now that three of my children have flown the nest. I have a pouring area, painting area, sewing room, and office . . . so why do my projects still overflow into other areas of the house? Alas, it is the curse of anyone associated with this wonderful hobby. We are true collectors of other people's discarded junk because "you never can tell when you'll need that."

Realistically, most dollmakers are cramped for space and simply do not have the luxury of taking over a spare bedroom. (Let's face it, you simply cannot put your thirteen-year-old out on the street no matter how much you need that doll room.) So where does one go with all her dollmaking paraphernalia when there is no room to spare? Take a good look around your house or apartment. A corner of the basement, laundry room, or even a spare closet could be turned into a great work area. Thee dollmaker's needs are relatively simple . . . good lighting, cleanliness, and comfort.

An essential requirement is adequate **good** lighting. The work area must be lit well to avoid shadows. This is especially important when painting. The work area must be kept clean. Cleanliness is indispensable both for good dolls and for the dollmaker's health. Comfort is the third consideration. The work surface should be at a comfortable height, and suitable seating should be available. Your dollmaking area should be warm in winter and cool in summer.

Probably you will perform the various dollmaking chores in different locations in your home. The casting area need not be elaborate. A section of heavy-duty shelving to hold molds, slip, buckets, and tools, and a casting table are all you need have. It is an added plus if there is a water tap convenient to the casting area. Always keep a bucket of water and sponge available for cleanup, and get in the habit of wiping everything down after each casting session to eliminate porcelain dust from being tracked all over the house.

The area necessary for firing can be quite small. Read the chapter on kilns to insure safe placement, adequate ventilation of the kiln, and safe storage of any products used in firing.

China painting is, for many of us, the best facet of dollmaking. Again, observe the basics of cleanliness, comfort, and adequate lighting. Remember, too, that china paint can be hazardous if handled improperly. I am well aware that the kitchen table may be the most logical area for china painting. Just don't eat or drink while you are painting.

A number of storage options are available for your china painting and other dollmaking supplies. Tool and/or tackle boxes are convenient for holding china paints, media, brushes, and other tools; and there is a multitude of covered, see-through plastic containers in shapes and sizes for every dollmaking need.

Remember, your work area can be as simple or elaborate as necessity dictates; but if kept clean and orderly, well lit, and comfortable, your dollmaking hobby will be much more enjoyable, both for you and those other folks you share the house with.

3 Porcelain

EARLY DOLLS WERE MADE by rolling out slabs of porcelain clay and pressing them into plaster molds. Around 1870, German dollmakers developed a method of mixing the clay in a more fluid consistency which could be poured into plaster molds. This liquid porcelain, called slip, was then drained from the mold when a suitable thickness of clay was attained. By the 1890s, almost all French and German doll heads were poured heads.

Today porcelain slip has been developed and improved to make slip casting easy for both hobbyist and professional. Porcelain slip is made up of clay particles (kaolin and other clays), water, and a deflocculant. The deflocculant is necessary to keep the clay particles in suspension (keep slip from separating). Seeley's porcelain slip casts, sets up, and releases easier and faster, shrinks less (Seeley's French Bisque only 13.6%), and produces stronger greenware and bisque than any other porcelain I've worked with. It comes in an abundance of colors, both for dollmaking and lace draping and other ceramic work. The projects in this book are making use of Seeley's French Bisque, Lady White, French Chocolate, and Aztec Tan; however, there are other porcelain colors you'll want to experiment with.

Seeley's Palette of Porcelain Colors for Dollmaking

PS1 Seeley's French Bisque® - world's best-known skin-tone slip for dolls.
PS2 Bone White™ - very strong, creamy white slip for figurines and ornaments.
PS3 Pearl White™ - white, translucent slip for dolls and figurines.
PS6 Brown Velvet™ - rich brown tone for black dolls.
PS8 Dresden Flesh™ - lighter skin tone than Seeley's French Bisque.
PS9 Oriental Flesh™ - warm, oriental skin tone.
PS10 Indian Flesh™ - rich, terra cotta tone.
PS17 Lady White™ - especially developed for dolls painted with overall wash.
PS19 French Chocolate® - creamy mellow chocolate tone for lighter brown and ethnic dolls.
PS21 American Bisque™ - healthy skin tone, ideal for modern dolls.
PS23 Aztec Tan™- sun-kissed golden skin tone.
PS24 Nordic White™ - blue-white, a match to many antique dolls.
PS25 Pure White™ - whitest white for dolls and figurines.
PS26 Naturelle™- Natural skin tone for modern and artists' dolls; also a base for ethnic dolls with overall wash.

Slip Casting

Slip casting is the process of pouring porcelain slip into a mold to create a casting of that mold. Most dollmakers simply refer to this process as *pouring*. Before beginning this adventure in pouring, take a moment to gather a few supplies.

Pouring Equipment

Porcelain slip in color of your choice
Molds

- Soft duster for cleaning out molds
- Plastic bucket
- Adequate rubber bands
- Sturdy wooden stir stick
- Large plastic pitcher
- Fine mesh sieve or pantyhose for straining slip
- A timing device
- Bucket of water, sponge and towel for cleanup
- Plastic mold cleaning tool
- Flexible straw or piece of ¼" plastic tubing

Let's begin. First, remove your jewelry; jewelry can damage castings. It might also be advisable to trim long fingernails as it is very easy to gouge greenware with long nails. For those of you who hesitate sacrificing your nails, try surgical gloves; they offer some protection. You may wish to cover your work table with layers of newspaper or paper towels to make clean-up easier.

Ideally, one should mix porcelain slip the night before pouring. By doing this, the bubbles have a chance to dissipate. It is nearly impossible to open a full gallon of slip and stir it in the container. It is much easier to pour the slip, strained through pantyhose or a sieve, into a wide-mouth plastic bucket for easier stirring. Stretch pantyhose over the bucket or use a sieve to catch any dry particles of clay that might be around the lid of the jar and also to break up any clay lumps. Always use a plastic bucket because a metal bucket could introduce rust into the slip, and the iron oxide would contaminate your casting, resulting in a wasted head.

Pour the slip into a wide-mouth plastic bucket.

Use a sturdy wooden dowel or paint stirrer to stir the slip. The slip must be stirred well, yet care must be taken not to beat the slip, as to do so will result in the formation of air bubbles. Air bubbles will result in pinholes in the casting. Pour the stirred slip into a container suitable for easy pouring; I find a large plastic pitcher convenient. The handle makes it easier to hold, and the spout is very handy for directing the flow of slip into the mold.

Before pouring, open the molds and gently dust them out with a mold dusting brush or other **soft** brush. Next, band the molds adequately using enough rubber bands or nylon mold straps. If the mold was previously poured with a darker slip such as French Chocolate or Brown Velvet, gently wipe it out with denatured alcohol and a soft cloth before banding.

Believe it or not, we are ready to pour. In the case of a head mold, it is preferable to tilt the mold slightly, allowing the slip to run down the back of the head. Tilting the mold and pouring the slip down the back of the head prevents the formation of "hard spots," which sometimes form when the slip repeatedly strikes the same spot in the mold.

Fill the mold with a smooth, steady stream of slip.

It is very important to **pour in a smooth, steady stream** as fast as possible to completely fill the mold to the top of the pourhole. Pouring too slowly or stopping momentarily will cause what is known as "hesitation lines." This phenomenon shows up as concentric rings around the casting, and these marks are impossible to remove. Always make sure you have enough slip to completely fill the mold. Top off the slip in the pourhole as the level recedes. **Do not** allow the level of slip to sink beneath the pourhole, as it would produce a thin, fragile area or even an incomplete casting. Now, allow the mold to set undisturbed until the casting has reached the desired thickness.

Completely fill the mold and keep it "topped off."

Drain the mold when the casting is 4mm thick.

As a beginner, you will want to time the set-up time of your various molds and keep a log for future reference. Watch the edge of the pourhole. When the clay wall has reached the thickness of one to two nickels (3 to 4mm), drain the remaining slip from the mold. To easily gauge the thickness of the casting, use a plastic cleaning tool to cut into the casting at the pourhole. It is not possible to state precise set-up times, as this timing is influenced by various factors. Size of the mold, the plaster quality and density of the mold, porcelain slip used, temperature of the room, mold and slip, humidity or lack of it, and moisture content of the mold will all influence set-up time. For instance, pouring in your basement next to the furnace will undoubtedly result in rapid set-up time, while pouring the same mold in a cool room on a rainy day will require a much longer set-up time. Likewise, if one used very viscous slip (thick and syrupy), set-up time will be swift, while watery slip will set up slowly. A wet mold will set up slowly while a dry mold sets up fast. Also, keep in mind that a small mold need not be poured as heavy (thick) as a large mold. Larger molds need to be poured heavier so the casting will be thick enough to support itself during cleaning and firing and be strong enough for stringing.

Blow into the mold as it is draining to keep the casting from collapsing.

Molds which have large pourholes will drain easily on their own. Drain the excess slip slowly, holding the mold at an angle to ensure that air replaces the slip as it drains from the mold. An ominous "glugg-glugg" sound indicates the creation of a vacuum inside the casting which may very well pull the casting away from the wall of the mold. This will appear as a caved-in area when you open the mold. To prevent this from happening, you need to force air into the mold cavity by using a flexible straw or piece of plastic tubing and lung power to blow air into the mold at the same time you are draining it. Remember to blow, or you may end up with a mouthful of slip; and take care not to poke the straw or plastic tubing though the side of the casting. After draining completely, allow the mold to remain upside down, propped on one side to permit air to circulate.

Prop the drained mold upside down for air circulation.

Housekeeping

The casting area must be kept clean to eliminate porcelain dust. Get in the habit of cleaning the casting area after each use. Wipe down the area with water. Porcelain drips and spills become porcelain dust when dry. **Do not put clay down the drain.** This is especially important if you have a septic tank.

Special Problems

All-bisque dolls and other molds of small body parts do require a bit of special handling. Very tiny molds pour best if the slip is thinned to a medium cream consistency with a teaspoon or two of **distilled water.** Stir the distilled water into the slip gently to avoid creating air bubbles. If you add too much water, castings will lose their inherent strength and resiliency and be more difficult to work with. Very watery slip will also cause your molds to become waterlogged.

An ear or glue syringe or some type of squeeze bottle is handy to force slip into tiny openings. Do not attempt to pour a group of tiny molds all at once. Set-up is rapid (two to three minutes), and the wee arms and legs will become solid before you can drain them if too many pieces are poured at once. You can pour a few large molds and then a small mold. Empty the molds in the reverse order in which you poured them - smallest to the largest. If the slip does not drain easily, use a cocktail straw to blow out the slip. Very tiny all-bisque dolls that will be "pegged" may have their arms and legs poured solid.

Head-torso dolls can be difficult to drain completely. Slip often remains trapped in the head because the narrow diameter of the neck retards draining. When draining a head-torso doll, make certain the head has emptied by using a flexible straw or plastic tubing to gently blow air into the mold as described earlier to aid draining.

Bent arms and legs can be troublesome to pour and drain. Holding the mold on an angle with the pourhole elevated sometimes helps these molds to fill. Immediately after filling the mold, use the heel of your hand to give the mold a "thump" or two on the side. This aids in getting trapped air pockets to fill with slip. Keep the contours of the mold cavity in mind when draining bent arm or leg molds. These pieces can not be drained straight up and down, but must be drained on an angle to insure that the slip drains from the lower half of the extremity.

Shoulder plates should be poured heavier as they warp easily. Shoulder plates should be poured thicker than other castings (large ones up to 5mm thick).

Reclaiming Slip

The word about reclaim is **don't** use it - discard it. Reclaim is the clay trimmed from the spare, eye cuts, head opening, etc. Some people reconstitute this and use it again. This reclaimed slip contains minute pieces of plaster as well as other debris picked up while casting, removing, and trimming the casting. In short, reclaim is contaminated and will be more costly in the end when you are left with less than perfect heads.

Reclaim **can** be used to pour a mold for the first time. Normally first castings of a new mold are discarded because some residual plaster in a new mold may be picked up by the first casting. These castings could be used to size the eyes for future reference. After firing, use a permanent marker to note eye size, wig size, body size, etc., directly on the head. As well, you could use Seeley's French Bisque or Lady White reclaim to clean out the residue left from casting a highly-colored slip such as French Chocolate, Aztec Tan, Brown Velvet, or Ebony.

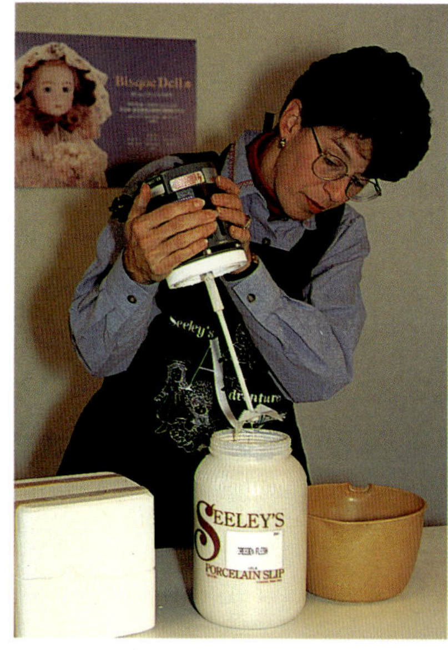

An electric mixing unit blends slip for pouring.

Optional Pouring Equipment

As your pouring ability and mold inventory increase, you may wish to add some equipment to make slip preparation and casting and draining of your molds faster. The **Slip Whiz** is an electric slip mixing unit designed to screw right onto the gallon slip container. Its stainless steel blades blend the slip to a smooth, creamy consistency with **no bubbles.** A larger unit, the **Flow Baby,** not only blends the slip in its own four-gallon container but pumps the slip through a five-foot-long hose to a faucet-type nozzle for easy mold filling. Draining molds is easier with a **Table Top Drainer.** This unit has removable wooden rungs over a six-gallon capacity fiberglass container. Molds can be placed atop the rungs to drain slip easily, and air can circulate freely beneath the mold.

4 Removing and Trimming the Casting

THE CASTING CANNOT BE REMOVED from the mold until it is firm enough to support its own weight without warping. The majority of warpage results from premature removal of the casting. Patience is a virtue when working with porcelain. Porcelain is not a particularly plastic clay. It has been said that porcelain has a memory. If you dent or warp the casting by pulling it out of the mold, it will revert to that condition after firing in spite of any attempt to reform it.

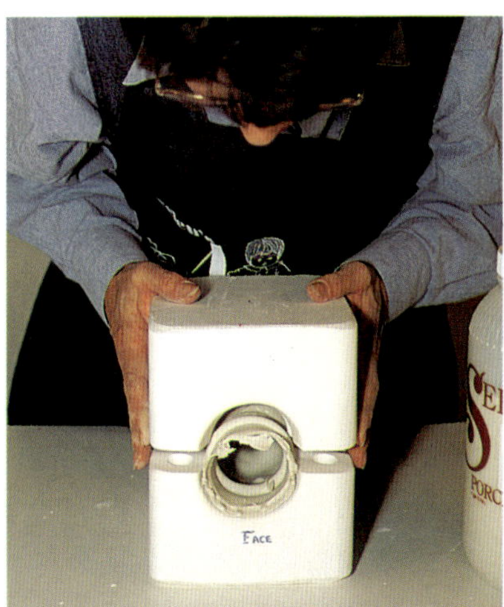

While waiting for the molds to open, use a mold cleaning tool to remove any slip drips or spills from the sides of the mold. Run a plastic mold cleaning tool between the clay wall of the spare and the mold. Molds should open easily without forcing. Forcing a mold could cause the casting to rip along the seamline. Remember, the wetter the mold, the longer it will take to open. Unband the mold, and attempt to remove the back half of the head mold first. Lift the mold straight up so as not to damage the soft casting. If the mold does not open easily, put it aside and try again later.

Leave the casting in the open mold for fifteen to thirty minutes

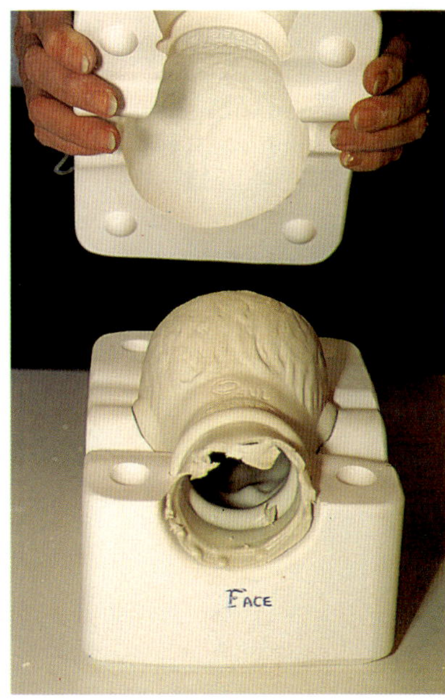

before attempting to remove it. Then allow the casting to gently fall out of the mold into your hand so that it is face up. Very large heads and other castings will need to be lifted out of the mold. When opening shoulder

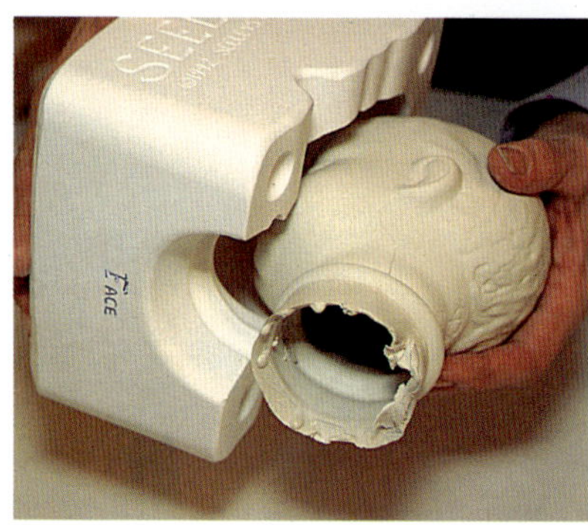

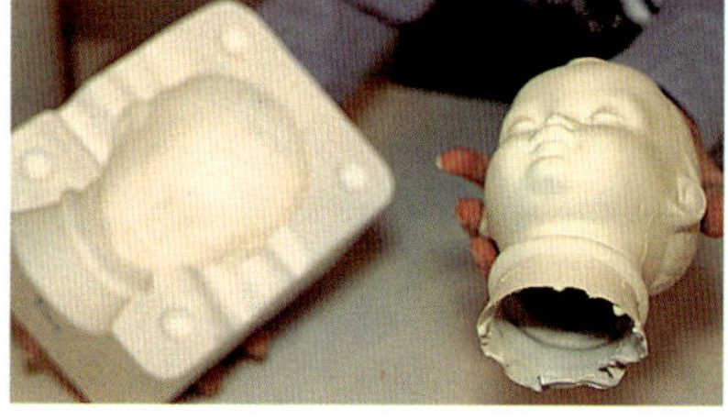

plate molds, allow the shoulder plate to remain in half of the mold to become firmer before attempting to pierce sew holes and doing any trimming. Warped shoulder plates are a problem for many dollmakers, and most warpage is caused by the impatience of the pourer.

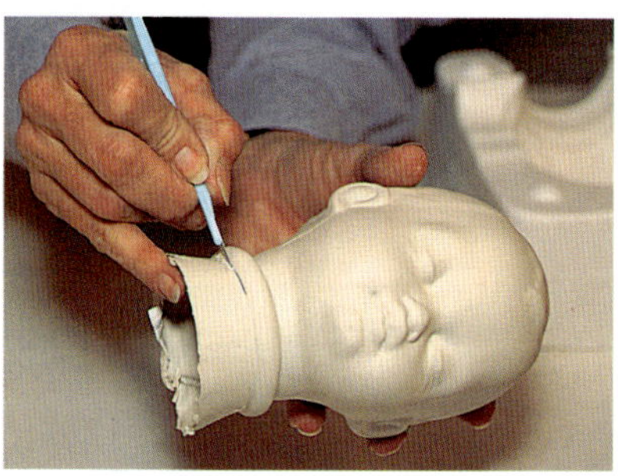

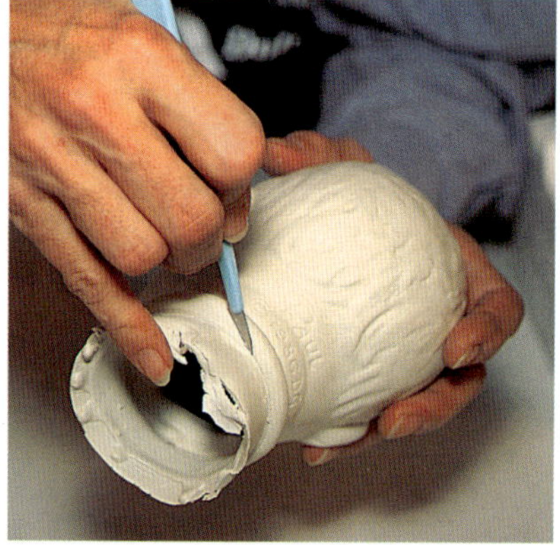

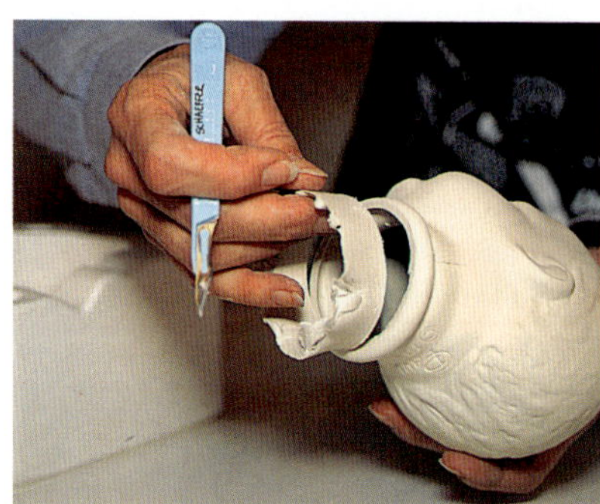

While holding the casting, use a sharp Featherknife or scalpel to remove the spare (the pourhole extension). Examine the surface carefully for pinholes or any other scratches or imperfections. Smoothing flaws with a moist, soft brush at this time will save headaches later.

Eye and Mouth Cutting and Ear Piercing

When doing antique reproduction dolls, it is imperative to have one or more good close-up photos of the antique doll to determine shape and size of eye and mouth cuts, the presence of teeth cut into the casting, and whether earring holes are pierced into the head or through the lobe.

The eyes are said to be the windows of the soul, and the eyes of a doll are often noticed before anything else. If eyes are cut poorly, the doll's beauty is destroyed.

Before cutting the eyes, measure to see that they are even. It is important to compensate for eyes that are uneven in size or place-

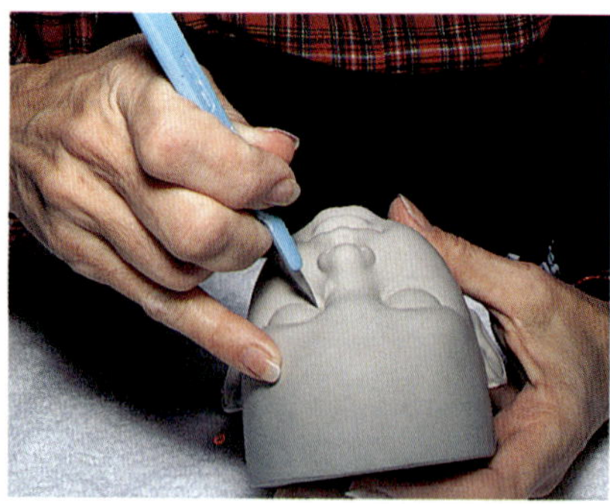

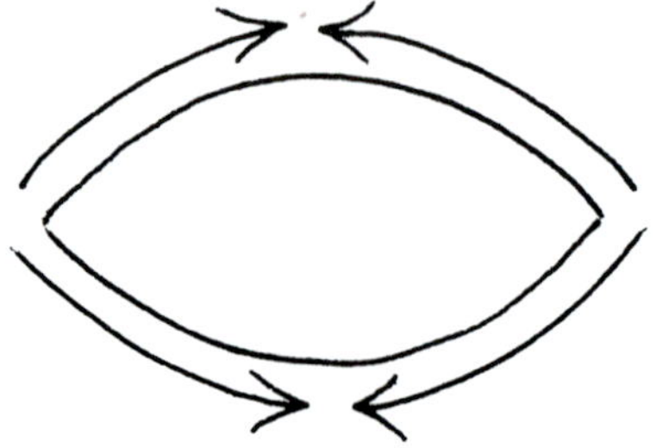

ment. Now use a sharp Featherknife, and cut the eyes as per the diagram. Do not use a sawing motion, as this will produce jagged edges which will easily chip when sizing the eyes. Cut from corners to center to avoid over cutting the corners.

The mouth opening is cut the same way; however, the corners of the mouth are rounded.

Ear piercing may be accomplished with a wet doll finger tool or small knitting needle. Ear piercing should be done as soon as the casting is removed from the mold. If the casting is allowed to dry too long, cracking of the ear lobe may occur.

The head pate is left in place until all other necessary work has

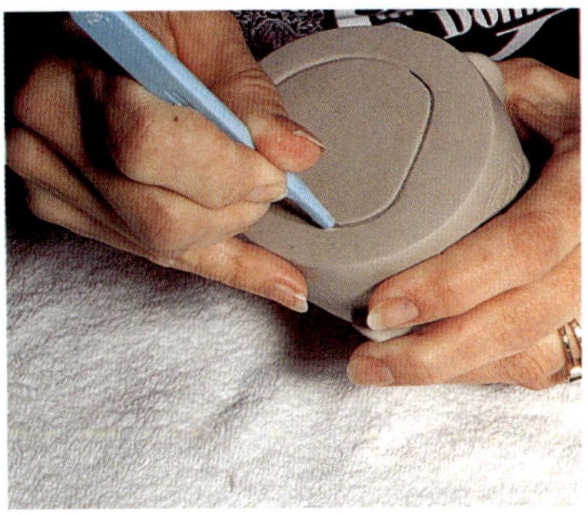

been completed. Then use a sharp Featherknife to cut out the head pate, taking care not to warp the

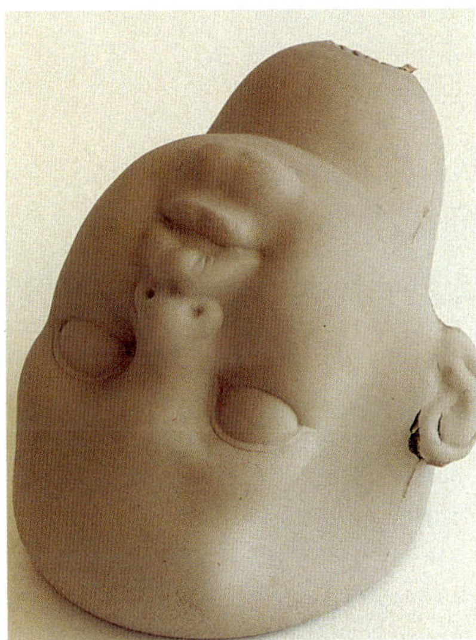

The casting will warp if it is handled while wet.

head. On very large heads, it is advisable to only score the head pate and remove it later when the casting has become harder, to avoid warpage.

Leave the castings to thoroughly dry in a well-ventilated area.

Patching

A number of small, all-bisque dolls require patching of the pourhole and/or the arms and legs.

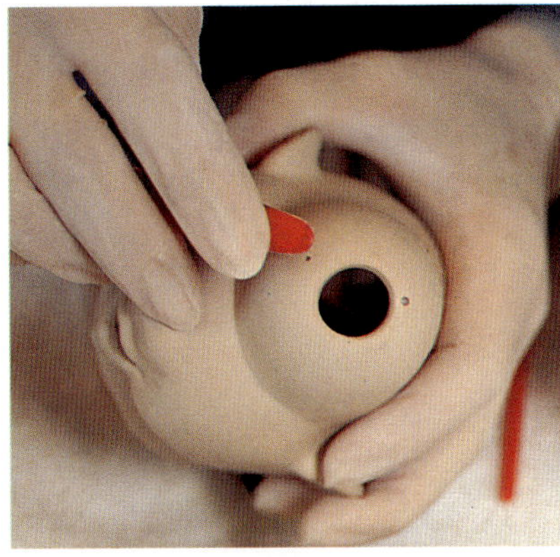

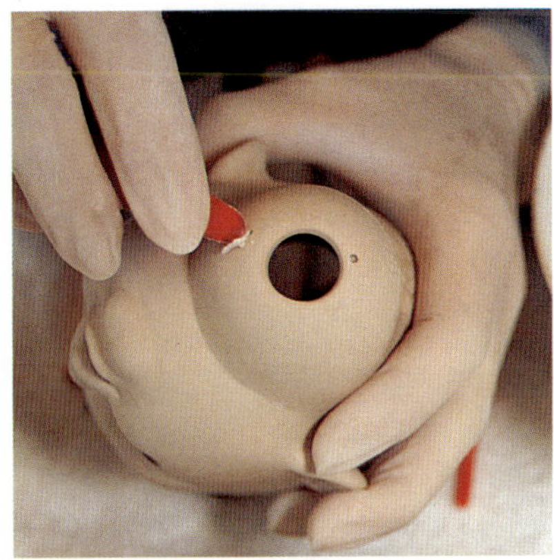

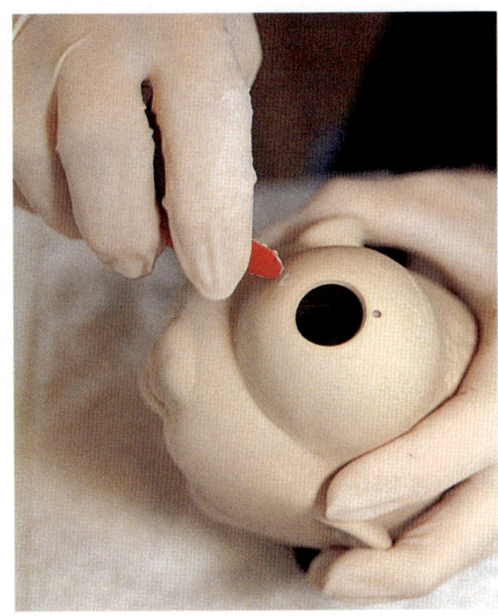

To make the patch, pour a small puddle of slip slightly larger than the area to be patched onto the outside of a mold. The plaster of the mold will absorb the excess moisture from the slip. Use a brush to "paint" slip around the pourhole; then, while the patch is still damp yet firm enough to be handled, pick it up with a palette knife, and place it over the hole to be patched. The wet slip acts as "glue" to hold the patch in place. Use a soft, damp brush or silk sponge to smooth the area.

Dust-Free Cleaning Technique

One of the most revolutionary changes in porcelain dollmaking was the introduction of The Dust-free Cleaning Technique. In my life before dollmaking, I was a registered nurse, and so I immediately welcomed this healthier, less hazardous method of cleaning wet porcelain. Fine silica powder, when inhaled, remains in the lungs forever, and eventually, if one breathes enough of it, he or she will develop silicosis. The Dust-free Cleaning Technique effectively eliminates 100% of this dangerous dust, and your home will remain a whole lot cleaner. Another benefit of this technique is that the dollmaker will gain better bisque because imperfections are easier to detect and remove. Additionally, soft-firing removes the crusting that often forms on high spots on the casting, eliminates a lot of breakage, and minimizes warpage.

To prepare the greenware for dust-free cleaning, the pieces must be soft-fired. In simple terms, that means the greenware undergoes firing to a low temperature (1112° to 1922° F./600° to 1050° C.) during which time all water is driven out of the clay, and the form becomes strong and capable of being immersed in water without dissolving. This soft-firing process must be completed slowly, as fast firing could trap steam within the clay which would result in pimples after the bisque fire. During soft-firing, it is perfectly all right for pieces to touch each other, as it is only during vitrification in the bisque fire that pieces will fuse together.

Before soft-firing, take a damp sponge, and smooth both the cut-out pate area and the neck opening. It is easier and faster to do this chore now.

Soft-Firing Schedule

Orton Junior cone 018 in sitter
Low - 1 hour - peepholes open
Low - Medium - 2 hours - peepholes open
Medium - peepholes open, until kiln shuts off

When kiln shuts down, close peep holes until kiln cools down completely
Breast Plates - use Cone 017 in sitter
(Because of their shape, breast plates crack easily, and a hotter fire will make them stronger.)

Your soft-fired porcelain is now ready to be cleaned wet.

Supplies:

- Small bucket with tepid water
- Eye-sizer tools covered with a thin, round make-up sponge, then nylon stocking material or fine nylon net held in place with a rubber band.
- Vinyl surgical gloves (optional)
- Featherknife™
- Wet Scrubbers
- Super Doll Sponges™
- Various brushes
- Optivisor®
- Stylus

Submerse the soft-fired bisque in a bucket of tepid water for five to ten minutes. I have left heads in water overnight with no ill effects. Vinyl surgical gloves may be worn if you so desire.

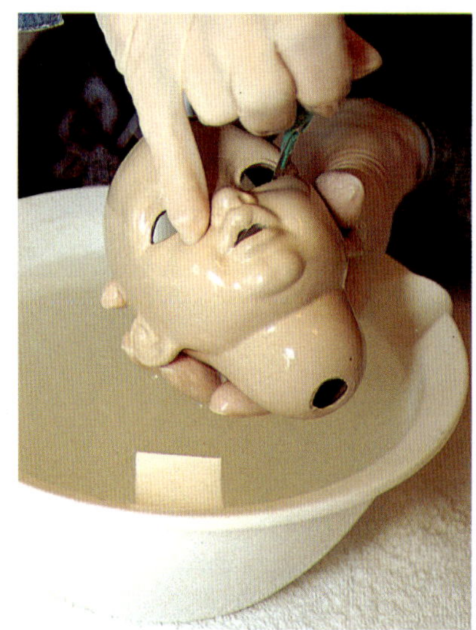

If the eyes were not cut out in the greenware, now is the time to open them up. Use a sharp, wet

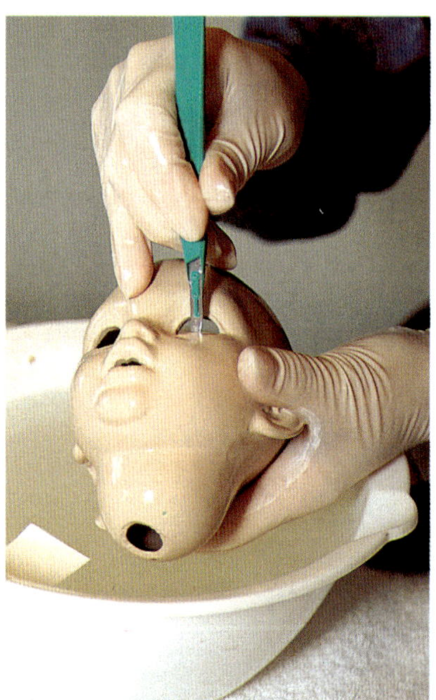

Featherknife to scrape out the eye shape. It is important to keep the area and the tools wet. Attempting

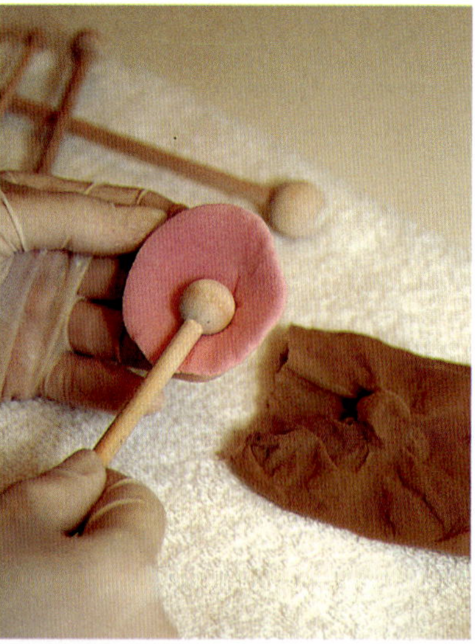

Cover the eye sizer with thin sponge and nylon.

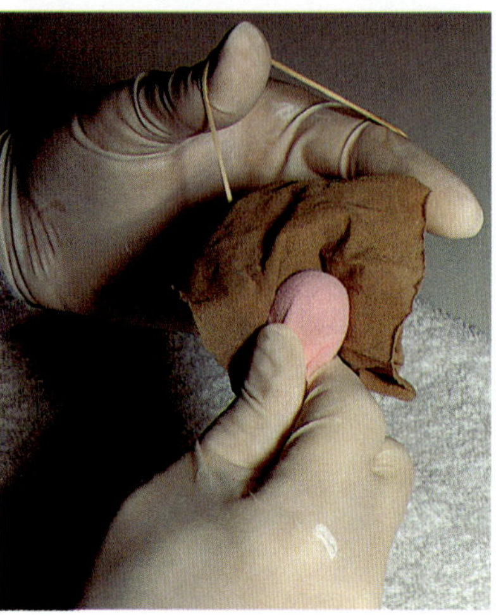

to cut the eye opening dry could cause the edges to crack.

I prefer to bevel the eyes before cleaning seamlines because if mishaps occur, it is usually during this process. Cover the proper eye sizer with a thin, fine, round make-up sponge, then nylon stocking material or nylon net. Keep in mind that the porcelain will shrink during the bisque fire; therefore, use an eye sizer, 2mm larger than the size you wish to end up with. (Example: the eye socket created by a 16mm eye sizer will accommodate a 14mm eye.)

Insert the WET, covered eye sizer into the head through the crown, and gently rotate it behind the eye opening to bevel the eye socket. It is important to hold the sizer straight behind the eye you are working on. If the eye sizer is held at an angle, one side of the eye socket will bevel deeper than the other. As paste and other debris accumulate, wipe it away with a wet doll sponge. It is imperative that you change your nylon stocking or nylon net material if it appears worn. If the ragged nylon stocking or nylon net material snags on the porcelain, it will cause the eye opening to chip. Use a wet nylon square shader brush to smooth any raw edges. Measure the eye opening frequently as you bevel to ensure symmetry. Go slowly until you get the feel for how

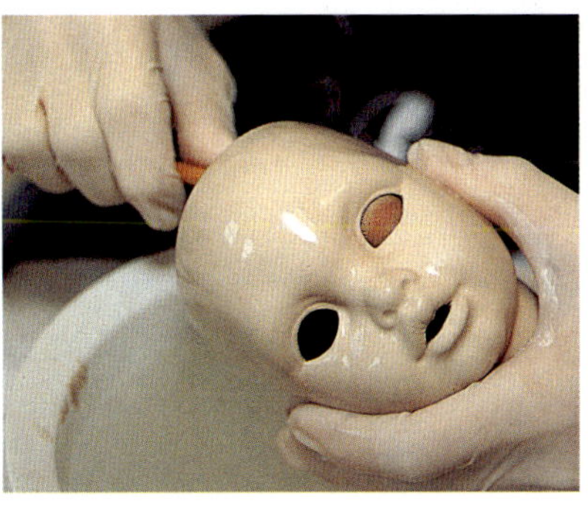

much pressure to exert. Beveling goes very fast, so be careful not to go too far. Alternate beveling, measuring, and smoothing until you have

two even, beveled eye sockets. You might wish to very gently try an eye in the eye socket to check the fit. Just be careful not to chip the fragile edges of the eye opening.

Next, take a small square (approximately 1" x 1") of Wet Scrubber, and with the rough side against the greenware, go over the seams in

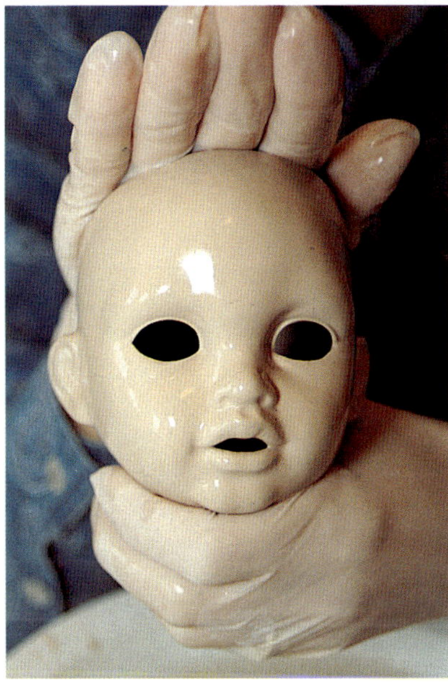

a circular motion. Be very careful to remove all traces of the seamline around the ears. The Wet Scrubber is a marvelous tool for cleaning soft-fired greenware, but it does its job very quickly; therefore, be especially careful around detailed areas so as not to flatten out or remove detail. As you remove the seams, a lot of paste-like debris will accumulate. Use a wet doll sponge to remove all of this debris. Use the small nylon square shader brush to do any necessary cleaning of the mouth, nostrils, or ears. Rinse the head well under running water, and use the doll sponge to make sure all cleaning scum has been removed.

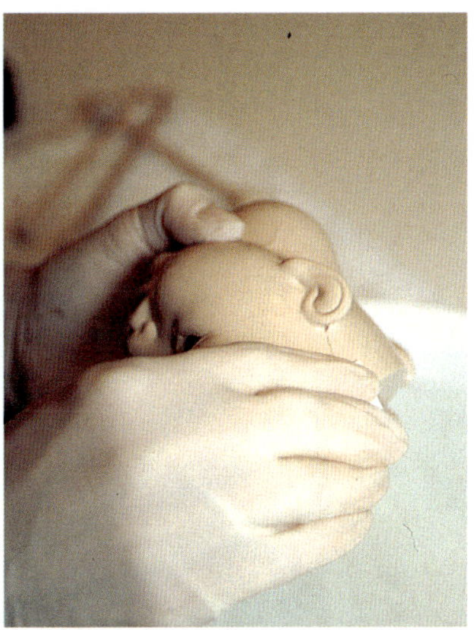

Use a Wet Scrubber with a circular motion to remove seam lines.

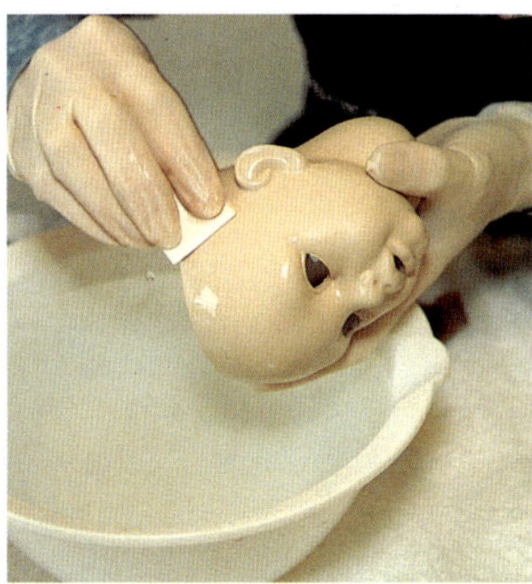

When you think you have finished cleaning the head, set it aside to dry off for a few minutes. It is difficult to see flaws on a wet, shiny surface; therefore, it is best to examine the head for imperfections **after** the water sheen disappears. Use an Optivisor or some other form of magnification to make sure that the head is as perfect as you can make it. Beautifully-painted heads begin with flawless greenware; therefore, put in extra time now in cleaning and inspecting your heads. Imperfections in the bisque appear much more obvious after china painting because tiny flaws "hold" the china paint, and therefore, they are accentuated. When you feel confident that you have removed all defects, use a Stylus to gently incise your name and the date on the back of the head, usually just below the mold mark.

Gently incise your name and the date on the back of the head.

5 The Kiln and Firing

KILNS AND THE FIRING process seem to frighten dollmakers more than any other facet of dollmaking. This chapter will, hopefully, alleviate those fears and get you well on the way to feeling comfortable with kiln operation. A kiln should not be viewed as a mysterious or dangerous object. On the contrary, the kiln is a necessary piece of equipment for the serious dollmaker who wishes to completely control the destiny of her doll. If used properly, with some common-sense safety precautions, the kiln is quite safe to use.

A kiln represents a sizeable investment, and therefore, you will want to do some planning and careful research before purchasing one. An often-asked question is, "Should I take a chance with a used kiln?" A used kiln is a lot like a used car . . . You'll never really know what it's been through and how hard it's been used (unless you can find a sweet little lady who only fired one china firing on Sundays!). Seek out a reputable dealer who will be available to help you with any problems that arise, and buy new, if at all possible. You'll get the necessary manuals and have a full warranty, not to mention help when you need it. An electric kiln is preferable for dollmaking. The size of the kiln you choose should be governed by how much firing you plan on doing. If you are an occasional dollmaker with little space for a kiln, you should look at a 110-volt kiln. I have a 110-volt kiln, which I use frequently for china paint test firings. If you plan on firing frequently, I would strongly suggest a small to medium 220-volt kiln with nichrome steel elements. A 220-volt kiln is necessary for repeated high firings (cone 6 and 7) and will be more efficient as well. Look for a kiln with a sturdy support stand and self-locking hinges on the lid. You will want to purchase a kiln equipped with a kiln sitter; and spending the extra money for a Limit Timer will prove to be a prudent investment.

The kiln sitter is a mechanical device that is operated with the use of a Junior cone. When the desired temperature has been reached, the partially-melted cone bends enough to trip the trigger which shuts off the kiln. The **limit timer** is an additional safety shut-off device, which will protect the kiln from overfiring (if the cone mechanism fails to operate) by

The kiln sitter (left) is a mechanical device that shuts off when the kiln temperature melts the cone inside. The limit timer (lower right) is an additional shut-off device, and it is based on time.

turning the kiln off at a preset time.

Kiln furniture will be needed to make full use of your kiln. Kiln furniture, made of refractory brick, consists of full and half shelves and posts in an assortment of sizes. Most kiln manufacturers have furniture kits available to fit their kilns.

Even before you purchase your kiln, you will want to give some forethought as to where it will be used. Keep in mind that the metal kiln jacket gets very hot. Place the kiln at a safe distance from walls and anything combustible. Kilns should be positioned a minimum of 12" from walls and furniture and away from draperies and curtains. The kiln, ideally, would sit on a concrete floor, but if that is not possible, a heat resistant material such as is used under wood stoves may be purchased from a hardware store. It is prudent to have the kiln as close to your source of electricity as possible. Running long electrical lines to the kiln is more costly initially for installation and makes the kiln less efficient to run. It is wise to have a professional electrician install and ground the proper receptacle for your new kiln. Another consideration in deciding where the kiln will be used is how the kiln will be vented. Placing the kiln on an outside wall will make proper ventilation easier.

Let's take a look at the kiln itself. The inside walls are composed of thick, refractory brick with horizontal grooves, in which are seated wire coils called **elements.** Electricity is conducted through these elements to heat the kiln. The larger the kiln, the more elements are required to heat it. Most kilns today have nichrome wire elements, composed of a patented alloy that withstands repeated high firings.

Inside the kiln: the elements are seated in wall grooves, the peephole allows oxygen to enter the kiln and vapors to escape during firing, and at left are the kiln sitter cone supports and sensor rod with firing gauge in place.

On the inside wall, you will also notice a porcelain tube from which extend the **cone supports** and the **sensing rod** of the kiln sitter.

The outside of the kiln is usually covered with a stainless steel jacket, and you will see one or more small round openings called **peepholes.** The peepholes allow oxygen to enter the kiln, allow vapors to escape during firing, and allow you to keep an eye on the firing by observing the witness cones.

Cones

The cone is a three-sided, pyramid-shaped or bar-shaped form made of ceramic material and used in the kiln to measure time and rate of heating and temperature during the firing process. In this book I use the three-sided pyramid-shaped Junior cone. There are two types of pyrometric cones.

Small Junior cones are used primarily in the kiln sitter. To insert a Junior cone, raise the weight of the kiln sitter up against the guide plate. Press the claw down until it engages the trigger, and insert the cone with the flat side resting on the cone supports and the sensing rod resting on top of the cone. Placing the Junior cone on the cone supports so that the thicker end lies under the sensing rod will produce a slightly longer and hotter firing, while inserting the cone so that the thinner end lies under the sensing rod produces a slightly shorter and cooler firing.

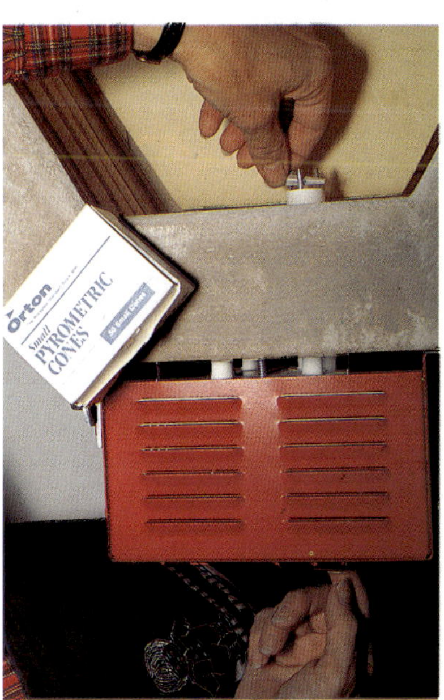

Insert Junior cone in kiln sitter.

Large witness cones or self-supporting cones measure time and rate of heating and temperature, the same as Junior cones, but these large upright cones are used on the kiln shelves. They make sure the kiln sitter is functioning properly and determine the hot and cool spots within the kiln. Ideally, witness or self-supporting cones are set up on a shelf in front of the peepholes. Three cones are used. One cone, the **Guide cone,** is one cone number cooler than the firing cone and will bend first as an early warning that the desired temperature to mature the ware is near. When this cone bends, you know the shut-off time is near. The **Firing cone** is next. It is the same number as the cone in the kiln sitter. After firing, a good bend for Seeley's French Bisque would have the cone bent at a 90 degree angle. The **Guard cone** comes next. It is one number hotter than the firing cone. This cone should remain upright - a bend to any extent indicates that the kiln is firing hotter than it should be.

The temperature achieved inside the kiln is determined by a number of factors. The amount of kiln furniture and its location and spacing, as well as the amount of ware being fired, will influence heat distribution in the kiln. Heat generally rises, and therefore, the bottom of the kiln will usually be a little cooler than the top; however, the opposite does occur in some kilns. Each kiln seems to have its own personality, and using witness cones throughout the kiln will help you understand the personality and quirks of your kiln.

Note: The small Junior cone will be bent harder than the large witness cone because the weight of the sensing rod will cause the softened Junior cone to bend at approximately one-half cone temperature earlier than the witness cone on the shelf.

Kiln Ventilation

During the firing process, a number of gases including carbon monoxide and sulfur-dioxide are

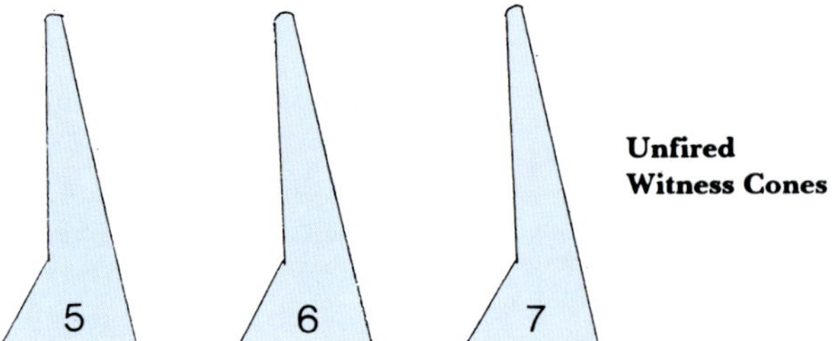

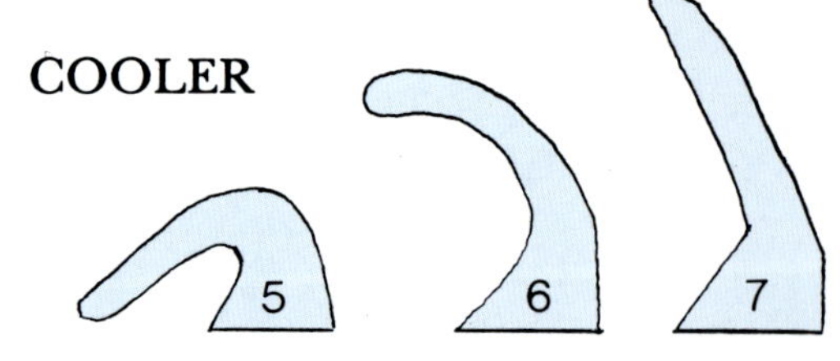

Witness cones should look like this after firing
French Bisque (PS-1)
Lady White (PS-17)
Bone White (PS-2)
French Chocolate (PS-19)
Indian Flesh (PS-10)
American Bisque (PS-21)
Aztec Tan (PS-23)
Oriental Flesh (PS-9)

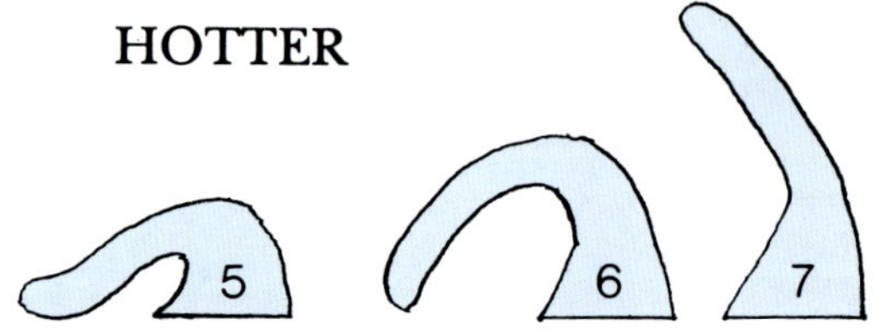

Witness cones should look like this after firing
Pearl White (PS-3)
Dresden Flesh (PS-8)
Nordic White (PS-24)
Pure White (PS-25)
Lady White (PS-17)

Firing Chart

Orton Jr. Cone (in the Kiln Sitter)		Orton Witness Cone (on the Kiln Shelf)
020	Some specialized china painting techniques	021
019	Lusters (Mother of Pearl, etc.)	020
018	Soft fire	019
017	Soft fire (Breast Plates)	018
016		017
015		016
014		015
013		014
0		
1		0
2	Glazes on porcelain	1
3		2
4		3
5	PORCELAIN FIRING	4
6	Lady and Bone Whites and colored slips (French Bisque, French Chocolate, Aztec Tan, etc.)	5
7	Pure White, Nordic White, Dresden Flesh, Lady White	6
6		7

Soft Firing & Overglazes: 020 019 018 017 016 015 014
Low-Fire Clays & Glazes: 06 05 04
High-Fire Porcelain: 1 2 3 4 5 6 7

Cooler ← → Hotter

released. It is essential that precautions are taken to vent these potentially hazardous fumes to the outside. An open window, door, or ventilating fan will remove a great deal of these fumes and vapors. Even better is a patented **Kiln Vent** system, which uses down-draft ventilation to pull fumes and odors through holes in the bottom of the kiln and discharges them to the outside via a dryer exhaust duct.

Loading the Kiln

It is essential that there be sufficient space around ware during the firing process to ensure even heat treatment; therefore, never fire ware directly on the bottom of the kiln. Instead, support a shelf on ½" to 1" posts, evenly spaced on the bottom of the kiln, and begin loading from there. A space of about 1" should be maintained between the shelf and the sides of the kiln. This much space is necessary to allow for proper heat treatment, the free venting of any gases produced during firing, and to give the operator room to get his/her hands in to remove or add a shelf. Special care must be taken not to place kiln furniture or ware too near to any part of the kiln sitter. To do so might jeopardize the operation of the kiln sitter. Additionally, kiln furniture and ware should be placed no closer than 1" from the kiln elements.

Loaded kiln shelves with bisque nestled in Firing Sand. Note witness cones on top shelf.

When loading heads and other items, load the kiln in a balanced manner. Distribute large and small items evenly to ensure that all pieces receive the same amount of heat. Likewise, allow space to remain between all pieces. During a bisque firing, this is a necessity lest one piece adhere to another during vitrification. Always place heads on shelves with their faces turned toward the center of the kiln.

When adding another shelf, be sure there is at least one element between shelves and between the last shelf and the kiln lid to ensure adequate heat in each section.

While loading, remember to position large, self-supporting witness cones on each shelf 2" to 3" behind the peepholes.

Separators and Support Products

The dollmaker uses various products in the kiln, both for support and to enable the porcelain to move on the shelf as it shrinks during firing. Which to use? This is usually dictated by individual preference. I recommend that high-fire kiln wash be applied to clean shelves and to the kiln floor, and I also use another separator on top of that. In addition to kiln wash and a separator, I occasionally use loose prop to keep large baby arms, legs, and the openings in all bisque bodies from warping out of shape. Whichever product you choose to use, remember that kiln wash is mixed with water and painted onto the shelves, while the aluminas and sand are sprinkled onto the shelves in dry form.

1. High-fire kiln wash: Kiln wash is a refractory material that prevents pieces from sticking to shelves. It is usually purchased in dry powder form and must be mixed with water to a heavy cream consistency. A coating of kiln wash is applied to the **top side** of each shelf and to the floor of the kiln with a wide paint brush. Kiln wash should never be applied too thick, or it will chip easily. To repair worn or chipped kiln wash, simply use a medium sandpaper to smooth any uneven areas, and recoat with another coat of kiln wash. A **thin** coat of high-fire kiln wash should also be applied to the top edges of the metal cone supports and the underside of the sensing rod of the kiln sitter to prevent cones from sticking.

2. Hydrated or Tabular Alumina: The aluminas are dry powders which, when placed on a kiln shelf (approximately 1/8" thick), act as a lubricant, which keeps the shrinking porcelain from "grabbing" the shelf during firing and so prevents warpage and cracking. Problems with hydrated or Tabular Alumina causing a "glazing" effect on porcelain bisque can be eliminated if one prefires the alumina by spreading it out on kiln shelves and firing it (by itself) several times to a true cone 6.

3. Silica Sand: Many dollmakers use sand for the same purpose and in the same manner as the aluminas. However, sand is not sand is not sand! When we talk about firing with sand, we do not mean sandbox sand, beach sand, or kitty litter! Large grains or uneven grains can cause pitting and scratching. Because the porcelain reaches an almost fluid condition during firing, it is easily damaged when it is pulled across the sand as it shrinks. The above sands also contain impurities and elements such as iron and manganese.

Seeley's sand, **Firing Sand**, is composed of smooth, round grains which act like tiny ball bearings that allow the porcelain to move freely while shrinking with no pitting or scratching. The Firing Sand does not have to be prefired.

The aluminas and silica sand are reusable. Whichever product you choose, please keep in mind that you do not need a ton of the stuff! Just because a little does a good job doesn't mean a lot will do a better job. All of these products are insulating materials; if one buries part of a neck, arm, or head in the material, the heat necessary to mature the porcelain may not get through. That buried portion of the porcelain head or limb may be underfired. A little goes a long way. A one-eighth-inch coating on the kiln shelf is sufficient. A half inch is usually all that is necessary to create a "nest" or pile to hold a dome head.

Eventually, you will be faced with difficult heads (often shoulder heads) and fat baby arms and legs that need extra support to prevent sagging. Two forms of prop are available:

1. **Loose Prop:** Loose prop looks much like cotton. It is composed of aluminosilicate fiber, which may be loosely molded to support heads and limbs during firing. Prop is also an insulating material, which means that if it is packed very tightly around a head or into a limb, it will prevent even firing, thus resulting in underfiring of the part protected by the prop. There is no need to stuff pieces tightly. Splitting occurs when one overstuffs legs and shoulder plates, because the porcelain shrinks during firing.

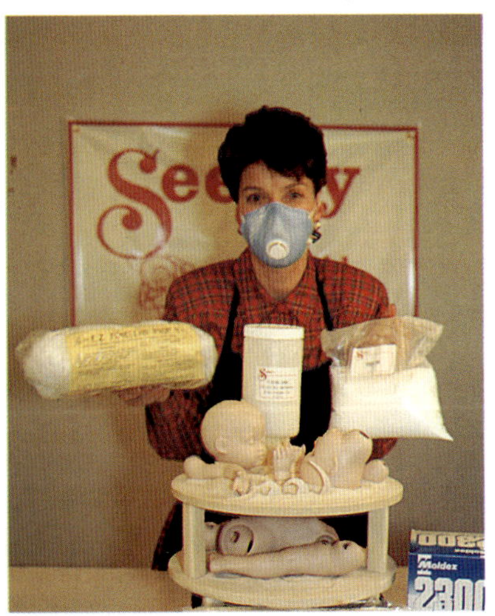

Separators and support products used in firing. Helen wears a respirator and gloves when she handles these products.

2. **Blanket Prop:** Blanket prop is made of the same composition as loose prop but is sold in compressed 12" x 24" sheets. Blanket prop may be used as is on the kiln shelf or cut to desired shape.

I do think it is necessary to discuss a few housekeeping and safety precautions which should be followed when working with the above products. Good housekeeping is essential with any of these products.

1. Read and follow the instructions accompanying any kiln product you use.

2. Store all kiln products in labeled, covered containers. Suitable inexpensive plastic containers are available in the housewares section of any discount store.

3. Place the substance you prefer to use on the kiln shelf (shelves) **before** being placed in the kiln. This cuts down on a lot of dust.

4. Hydrated or Tubular Alumina and Silica Sand must be kept away from the kiln elements. These products, if allowed to settle on the elements, cause them to become brittle and thus shorten the life of the elements in your kiln.

5. Develop the habit of vacuuming your kiln weekly. Use a soft brush attachment to remove any of these products which might have gotten on the elements.

6. Remove any of these products from the kiln shelves before china firing.

Please take some simple safety precautions when working with any of these products. All fine powders are dangerous to breathe. Whenever handling the aluminas or sand, get in the habit of wearing gloves and a respirator approved for toxic dusts and mists. Some of these products are composed of such fine particles that they remain in the lungs and could result in silicosis.

Bisque-Firing Schedule for Soft-Fired Ware

Colored, Bone and Lady White Porcelains - Junior cone 6 in sitter, witness cones 5, 6, 7, on shelf.

Other White porcelains - Junior cone 7 in sitter, witness cones 5, 6, 7, on shelf.

Medium - 10 minutes with lid open (to thoroughly dry ware)

Medium - 4 hours with lid closed, peepholes open

High - until kiln shuts off, peepholes closed

After firing, allow the kiln to cool down naturally before opening. **Thermal shock** occurs when the kiln lid or peephole is opened, allowing cool air to enter while the kiln is still very hot. Thermal shock can cause hairline cracks or even shattering of the ware. A good rule of thumb is to allow the same amount of time to cool the kiln as was required to fire it. **Never open the kiln during the firing or cooling down period.** When the kiln lid is no longer hot to the touch, it is safe to open.

Firing Log

Until you are thoroughly familiar with your kiln and can easily estimate firing times, it would be helpful and prudent to keep a written record of each firing. Use a notebook to write down date of firing, porcelain slip and batch numbers, cone number, witness cones used, type of load (bisque, china fire, etc.), amount of time on timer, firing time, and final appearance of cones used. This record will help

FIRING LOG

FIRING NUMBER	DATE	JR. CONE NUMBER	LARGE WITNESS CONE GUIDE	LARGE WITNESS CONE FIRING	LARGE WITNESS CONE GUARD	TYPE AND SIZE OF LOAD	TOTAL FIRING TIME HOURS	TOTAL FIRING TIME MINUTES	FIRING CONE APPEARANCE	REMARKS
1	12/7/92	6	5	6	7	BISQUE 3 SHELVES VERY FULL	9	45	WELL BENT	NO PROBLEMS
2										
3										
4										
5										
6										
7										
8										
9										
10										
11										
12										
13										
14										
15										

familiarize you with how much time is required of different types/sizes of loads and will help you get consistently good firings.

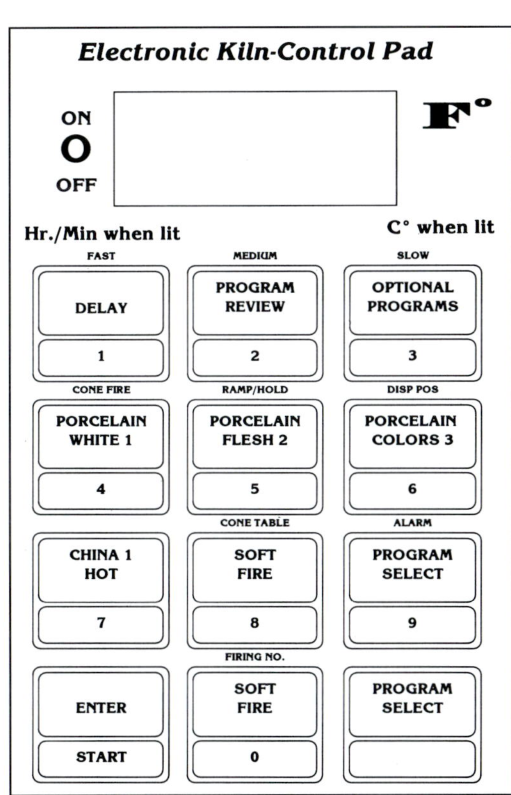

The control pad on this electronic kiln is pre-programmed to fire Seeley's porcelain slips and china paints. It has one-touch operation for soft firing, bisque firing and china firing.

Automatic Kilns

Completely automated, computer-controlled kilns are rapidly becoming a major portion of the kiln market. These kilns generally have a thumbwheel (calibrated from 1 to 10), which automatically increases power to the elements. When the firing is begun at the *1* setting on the thumbwheel, the elements cycle on 20% of the time and off 80% of the time. By the time the thumbwheel advances to *5*, the elements are on 50% of the time and off 50% of the time; and at *9*, all elements are on 90% of the time. The speed control may be set from a normal speed (a fairly fast temperature climb) to a slow speed (a slower heating rate).

Porcelain undergoes many changes during the bisque firing, and it is essential that the process is completed slowly. With that in mind, the slowest speed must be selected when bisque firing porcelain. I have had no untoward effects doing my china firings in a computerized kiln set at normal speed.

Select a slow firing speed for soft-bisque firings. The soft-bisque fire should last at least four hours.

One last word: all kilns are slightly different, so for best results, do read and follow **your** kiln owner's manual carefully.

Compare size of unfired greenware at left and right to fired bisque pieces in center.

Problem Solving

It is of utmost importance that your kiln fires to the correct temperature. The porcelain must be fully mature, yet not overfired.

Underfired porcelain has a chalky appearance. Porcelain that is underfired will develop a so-called "mildew" effect after china firing. It appears as blotchy, discolored areas of a myriad of tiny specks. Underfired heads can be salvaged. To do so, simply refire one cone cooler than your original bisque fire. You should be aware that if the head has been china painted and fired,

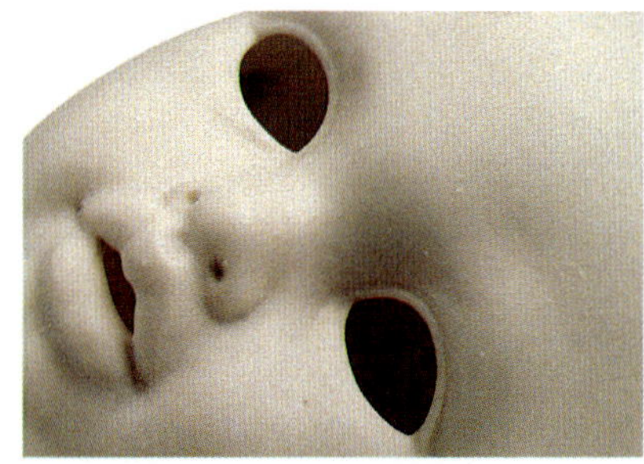

An indication of overfired porcelain is blistered or "pimpled" bisque.

colors in the red family will usually fire off; however, other colors will remain and may dramatically change

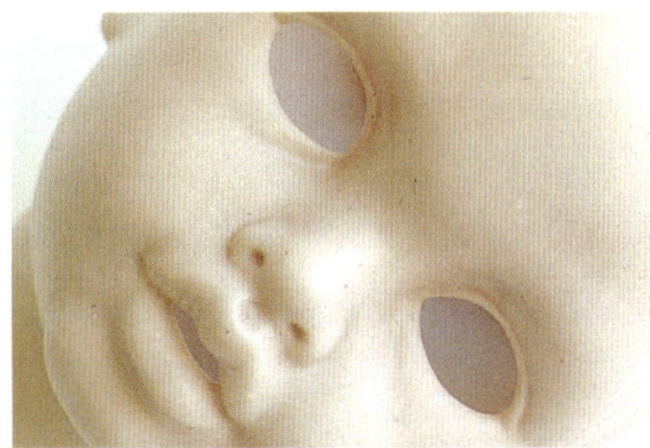

Tiny specks may develop on underfired porcelain.

at the higher firing temperature. Additionally, any Flux from the china paint will remain on the bisque after firing.

Overfired heads, on the other hand, are not salvageable. Dispose of them. Overfired porcelain appears quite shiny and has pimples or even blisters.

Don't take chances; get in the habit of using witness cones to check the accuracy of your kiln at least once a month.

Kiln Calibration. If you find that cones are not bending properly, it may be necessary to adjust the kiln sitter of your kiln. Relax, this won't hurt a bit! Remember that gadget you found on the kiln sitter when your new kiln arrived. (Hopefully your kiln dealer told you to keep it in a safe place.) This metal disk is called a firing gauge (see photo on page 19). Place this firing gauge in position over the sensing rod and the cone supports. With the firing gauge (sometimes referred to as calibration gauge) in place, lift the sitter weight up against the guide plate, and pull the claw forward. The tip of the trigger should just barely clear the claw of the kiln sitter. Check this function approximately every 30 days.

If the kiln is underfiring (firing too cool), raise the trigger by loosening the set trigger screw and moving the trigger up a millimeter or two. On the other hand, if the kiln is overfiring (firing too hot), lower the trigger by loosening the trigger set screw and moving the trigger down a millimeter or two. Make only a small adjustment at a time, and test fire the kiln after each adjustment. After making any adjustment, don't forget to re-tighten the set screw firmly.

Keep your kiln manuals in a safe place, and refer to them often.

6 All You Ever Wanted to Know about China Paint and The Waterbase Technique™

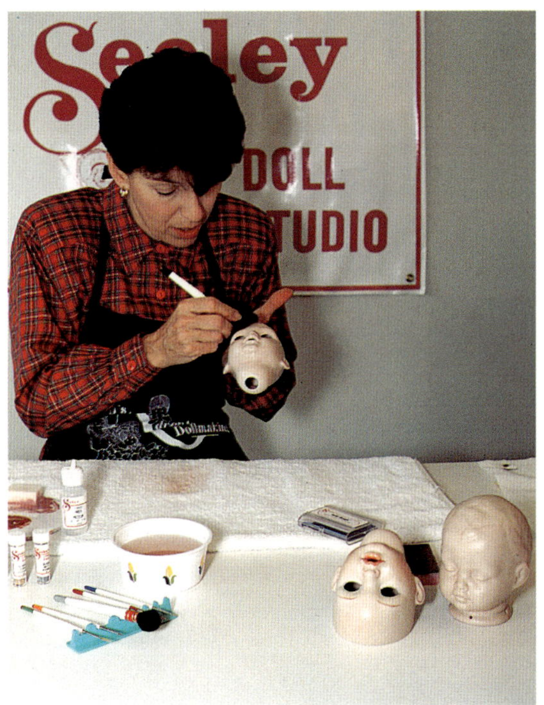

THE WATERBASE TECHNIQUE was developed in 1986 by Seeley's and the Doll Artisan Guild. As the name "Waterbase" implies, the foundation or base of the medium used to mix the dry china paint is a water-soluble medium.

Using water-based media has a number of advantages. As with most recent innovations in dollmaking, an important reason for recommending water-based media is a health consideration. Simply put, a water-based medium is "cleaner" to fire. Oil-based media must burn off during the firing process, resulting in the dollmaker being exposed to noxious fumes and a putrid odor. Aside from the definite health benefit of water-based media, they are also easier to work with to paint fine lines, blend color, and obtain different color values.

Many péople assume, incorrectly, that to paint with The Waterbase Technique, one must purchase all new china paints. Not so; the main difference between The

Waterbase Technique and the old, traditional oil-based method is the media used. Dry powder china paints may be mixed with any media; therefore, all that one need do to change from oil base to water base is to switch to water-based media and either replace or thoroughly clean your brushes.

We all know that water and oil do not mix; consequently, one can not use pre-mixed moist china paints with a water-based medium, as they have already been mixed with oil-based media. The exception to this rule is Seeley's Blush Pacs. These are china paint colors for cheek blush

Seeley's Blush Pacs

and eye shadow which have been pre-mixed with water-based media for your convenience.

Brushes used with water-based media must be free of any oil residue, as any oil remaining in the brush hairs would cause china paint mixed with a water-based medium to bead up when applied. If it is necessary to use a set of brushes that were used with oils, clean them thoroughly with an oil-cutting product such as *Fantastic*, and rinse well under running water.

Let's take a look at the different media employed when using The Waterbase Technique for china painting. All water-based media are odorless, nontoxic, and water soluble. They are, therefore, easily removed from your hands, brushes, and tile with water. Mistakes are also cleanly removed with water.

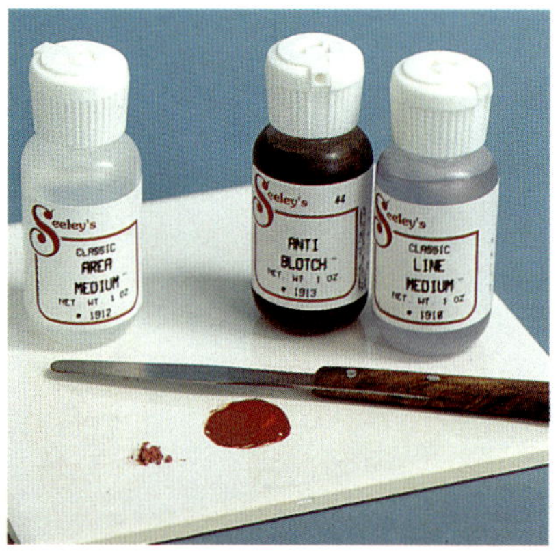

Dry (powdered) china paint is mixed with a water-based medium.

There are two primary media used in The Waterbase Technique to mix paint. **Area Medium (#1912)** is a colorless, **slow-drying** medium used to mix paint for large smooth areas of color such as overall (skin tone) washes, cheek and lid blush, and painted hair. In addition to mixing these colors with Area Medium, a thin film of Area Medium is also applied to the bisque before painting overall wash, cheek blush, eye shadow, and sometimes hair colors to make even blending of color easier. Area Medium is thinner than Line Medium and will dry off in time depending on the amount of moisture in the air.

Line Medium (#1910) is a lavender-tinted, thicker, non-drying medium used for mixing paint for fine lines and smaller areas such as eyelashes, eyebrows, lip and lip accent lines, and painted eyes. It enables the dollmaker to paint long, flowing lines of consistent color. Line Medium, like Area Medium, draws moisture from the air. Using Line Medium on a humid day may result in a watery china paint mixture, which would affect both the ease of application as well as the final color. Refer to "Mixing China Paints" for information on resolving this problem.

A secondary medium used in The Waterbase Technique is **Anti-Blotch (#1913),** which is an optional additive to Line Medium. Anti-Blotch, which is extremely fast drying, helps the painter apply a smooth coat of paint by altering the surface tension of the atmospheric water that is attracted to the Line Medium. This quality of Anti-Blotch makes it especially helpful when the humidity is high. As Anti-Blotch dries, it forms a skin, so one must take care not to over-stipple, over-blot, or otherwise overwork the paint containing this additive, as unsightly blotches will result. When Anti-Blotch is added to china paint, it must be added sparingly. A fraction of a drop is all that is needed.

Water, the other secondary medium, is the foundation upon which the entire Waterbase Technique is built. Water is used as a thinner of Area and Line Media and is used to condition brushes for china painting and for cleaning your brushes as well as removing any china painting mistakes.

Mixing China Paints

One of the biggest mistakes that the doll painter makes is mixing the china paint with too much medium, resulting in runny, overly diluted color. Mix dry china paint with a very small amount of medium

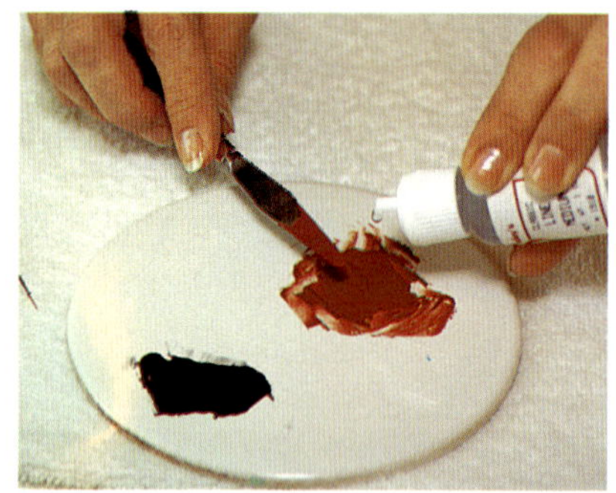

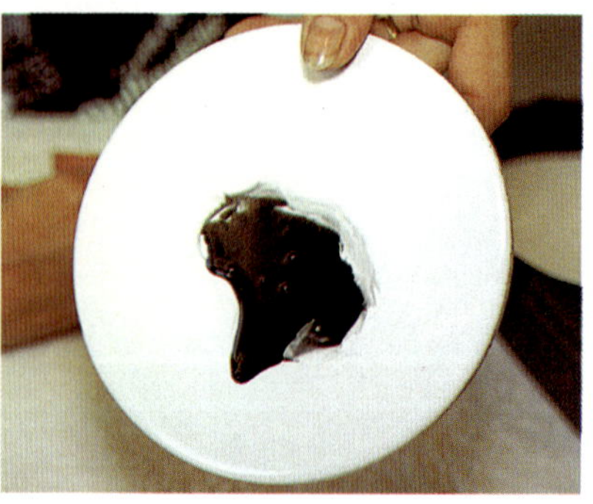

to a heavy paste consistency. Dry china paint is best mixed with the appropriate medium on a glazed or glass tile using a Palette Knife. Use a circular motion to grind the grains of china paint into the medium until the resulting mixture is very smooth. Small, unwanted dots of darker color (which usually do not show up until after firing) are the result of failing to grind the china paint sufficiently. After china paint has been mixed to a heavy paste consistency, allow it to stand for about fifteen minutes to see how much atmospheric moisture will be attracted to the medium. If the china paint is still too thick, add a bit more medium to achieve the desired cream consistency.

If handled improperly, china paints can be hazardous to your health because of their composition. Lead, which is an ingredient of most china-paint colors, is harmful when ingested or inhaled.

When mixing china paint, do so with care so as to create as little dust as possible. Remember to wash your hands thoroughly after china painting and especially before eating or smoking. Don't eat, drink, or smoke while china painting. Most important of all, **NEVER** put your brush in your mouth! Water or a little medium will put as nice a point on your brush as saliva! Mistakes are easily removed with a water-moistened cotton-tipped toothpick, a water-dampened Medium Area Brush, or Dolly Dough (a kneadable dough-like product that can be shaped to a fine point to "erase" or remove mistakes). Last but not least, do not allow children to handle china paints. Lead accumulates in body tissues, and little ones reach toxic levels rapidly.

This information is not meant to frighten you; it is simply good common sense to handle any potentially hazardous material with respect, and china paint is quite safe to use when used with care.

China Painting

China paints are known as overglazes because they are most commonly painted on top of a fired glaze, then fired to a temperature lower than the original glaze fire to fuse the color to the glazed surface. Because porcelain bisque is vitreous (non-porous), china paint can be painted and fired directly onto the bisque.

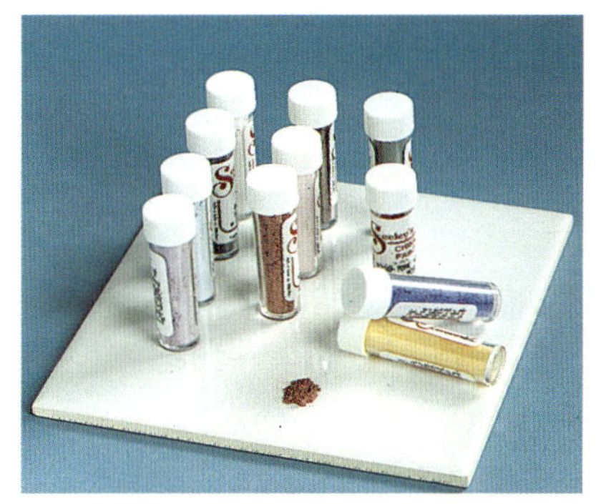

China paint is basically composed of finely-ground mineral colors (from metal oxides) and Flux and is available to the china painter in dry powder form in a myriad of colors. China paints are packaged in vials and are available for purchase either individually or in several convenient kits. Don't be fooled by the size of the vial. That small amount of china paint will last a long time, and because it is in dry form, it will never dry out or otherwise "go bad."

As mentioned earlier, several colors are also available in Blush Pacs. These are dry china paints that have been factory pre-mixed with water-based media. These ready-to-use china paints are packaged in convenient, round plastic containers with re-closeable lids.

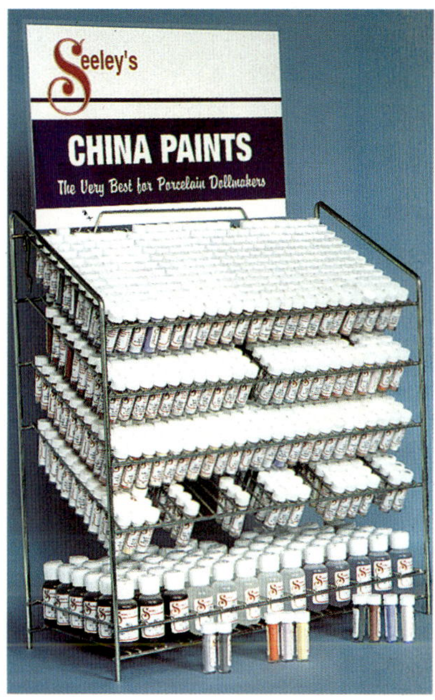

China Paint Firing Schedule

Junior cone range: 017 to 019 in the sitter (except dark ethnic dolls)

Initial wash - Junior cone 017 in sitter, 018 on shelf

Subsequent firings - Junior cone 018 to 019 in sitter, witness cone 019 to 020 on shelf

Fire Slowly

Keep peep holes unplugged during the entire firing:

One and one-half hours on **Low,** with lid propped,

Two hours on **Medium,**

Switch to **High.**

Seeley's Palette of Colors for the Dollmaker

The following china paint colors have been specifically formulated to color match the magnificent antique dolls of our past; however, they are equally superior for painting modern dolls. All colors listed here are gloss unless otherwise noted.

Overall Wash Colors

The overall wash colors are designed for use on white bisque. These colors are mixed to a heavy-cream consistency with Area Medium. The color is applied to bisque in a wiping motion and then polished smooth with a china mop.

DGBT01 Bisq-Tone #1
Creamy Rose - for French and some German dolls
DGBT02 Bisq-Tone #2
Raspberry - strong rose color with a touch of blue
DGBT03 Bisq-Tone #3
Apple Blossom - pale rose for pale French and Lady dolls
DGBT04 Bisq-Tone #4
Oriental - skin tone for Oriental dolls
DMBT05A Bisq-Tone #5
Early French - delicate pale, matt skin tone for early French and other pale dolls
DGBT06 Bisq-Tone #6
Peachberry - pink colored with a hint of blue, match for C-Steiner
DGBT07 Bisq-Tone #7
Peaches 'N Cream - soft peach, match to *Kestner's A. T.* Perfect for German dolls and French Brus

Eyebrow Colors

Eyebrow colors are mixed with Line Medium. The colors may be mixed together to achieve yet other variations.

DGEB01 Eyebrow #1
Toffee - light toffee with green tinge for blond dolls
DGEB02 Eyebrow #2
Olive Brown - medium greenish-brown for Jumeaux and Steiner
DGEB03 Eyebrow #3
Copper - coppery brown with hint of green, French, German and Baby
DGEB04 Eyebrow #4
Dark Brown - medium to dark brown, K★R, Simon & Halbig and more

Eyebrow Companion Colors

These are a match in color, but deeper in intensity, to be used as companions with Eyebrow Colors #1-4. For brow strokes, over strokes, and feathering. Can also be used alone.

DGEB01D Eyebrow #1D Dark Toffee
DGEB02D Eyebrow #2D Dark Olive Brown
DGEB03D Eyebrow #3D Dark Copper
DGEB04D Eyebrow #4D Dark-Dark Brown

Other Eyebrow Colors

DGEB05 Eyebrow #5
Topaz - Brown with touch of golden olive, match for *Jumeau Arielle*
DGEB06 Eyebrow #6
Dark Champagne - Brown with the most olive, match to *Kestner's A. T.*, also for Brus and other A.T.s
DGBR05 Mocha
Brown with olive tint for *Tête Jumeau* eyebrows or for perfect skin tone on brown Bru dolls
DGBR06 Mahogany
Reddish tone for eyebrows or good wash for brown Jumeau or Steiner dolls
DGBR07 Charcoal Brown
Charcoal colored for lashes
DGBR08 Rich Henna Brown
Strong reddish brown with a satin sheen. Wonderful for *A. Marque* and *Mein Liebling*
DGBR09 Chestnut Brown
Glossy red brown for brows and lashes on modern dolls
DGBR10 Smoky Topaz
Deep, dark brown that will hold color in fine strokes

Lip Colors

These colors are mixed with Line Medium to a creamy consistency. A fraction of a drop of Anti-Blotch will keep your color smooth.

DGR08 Rose Red
Soft rose tone for both French and, in many cases, German dolls. Great on modern babies
DGR04 Classic Yellow Red
Light orange-red for many German dolls and some late French dolls
DGR02 Pompadour Red
Medium to ruddy skin tone, also in matt for cheek blush
DGR03 Persian Red (Flesh)
Lighter skin tone; good for babies, also in matt for cheek blush
DGR13 Whispering Rose
Bright and intense rose for modern dolls as well as French and German, also as overall wash and blush

Cheek Blush Colors

DGCB01 Cheek Blush
Deep, red-rose color
DGCB02 Ruby Cheek Blush
Bolder cheek color for dolls with "apple" cheeks

These Cheek Blush colors are also available in pre-mixed (water-based) Blush Pacs.

Eye Shadow Colors

DMR06A Dusky Lilac
Pale lilac rose with gray tones. Matt lid blush for many French dolls
DGLM01 Lavender Mist
Strong lavender shade, more intense than Dusky Lilac, for eye shadow and eye painting modern dolls

Experiment with color when painting eye shadow on modern dolls. A touch of DGBL01 Light Blue makes a baby's eyelid almost transparent. For a dramatic look, try DGBL04 Royal Velvet, DGBL07 Slate Blue, or DGG05 Dark Avocado. For more depth, add a bit of brown. The possibilities are endless.

Additional Colors

DGB01 Black
Grayish-black gloss for lashes and pupils
DMB01 Black
Matt for lashes and pupils
DSB01 Satin Black
A satiny color, darker than Gloss Black and lighter than Onyx Black
DGB02 Onyx Black
A very black, black. Ideal for painted shoes; also lashes and lid lines on modern dolls
DGBR04 Russet
For baby hair and flesh toning on Modern Dolls, particularly young children
DGGR02 Pearl Gray
Creamy shade for body and facial contours
DGBL06 Teal Blue
Painted eyes, mixes well with other blues for eye shadows
DGBL07 Slate Blue
Lovely blue grey for painted eyes
DGBL08 Sapphire Blue
Vivid deep blue for modern dolls, chinas, parians, all-bisques. Mix with Slate Blue for painted technique
DSW01 Satin White
Very opaque white for eye highlights and clothing

Special Items

Matter

This is a matting agent which, when mixed with a gloss china paint, produces a matt effect.

Flux

Flux is a white powder which adds more gloss to china paint and helps fuse the color to the bisque when fired. Adding Flux to china paint will lighten the color, and one should never use more than one (1) part Flux to four (4) parts china paint.

7 Brushes: The Tools of the Trade

EVEN AS A CABINET MAKER cannot do good work with inferior tools, so a dollmaker needs quality brushes to create fine dolls. Are superior brushes expensive? Not really. Good brushes are an investment, and with proper care, they will last far longer than "bargain" brushes and save the user much frustration as well. There are two prerequisites in manufacturing a top-quality brush: the quality of the hair and the expertise of the brush maker. Yes, in these days of mass-production, quality brushes are still hand crafted by skilled and experienced craftsmen.

How can one tell a good brush from a bad one? First and foremost, a good brush should (with proper care) retain its shape. Brushes with splaying or bent hairs present a major annoyance. The doll painter wants and needs a brush with some spring or life to it. Did you ever try to paint a line with a floppy brush? The hair of cheap brushes is generally limp and not suitable for the kind of painting dollmakers do. Inferior brushes are never a bargain, and both the novice and the experienced dollmaker will paint better dolls with quality brushes.

Brushes are generally manufactured from natural animal hairs or a synthetic such as nylon. Synthetic brushes are able to take more abuse than those made of natural animal hair; however, there is a need for both types if one wishes to paint really beautiful dolls. Each of the brushes described in the following paragraphs have been designed to perform specific tasks when painting with The Waterbase Technique.

There are several synthetic brushes that one simply cannot paint dolls without. Synthetic brushes produce bolder, sharper lines. These brushes need to be reloaded after each stroke for consistent color.

The long, thin hairs of the **Eyelash Liner #1** (blue tip) make it an absolute necessity for painting lashes. The Eyelash Liner can be used as is, but trimming results in even finer lines. This brush can also be used to paint eyelid lines in painted-eye dolls and accent lines on lips.

Another necessary synthetic brush is the **Eyebrow Liner #2** (green tip), which is similar to the Eyelash Liner, only with longer hairs. This brush produces fine, sharp lines and is wonderful for the feathered eyebrows on many German dolls.

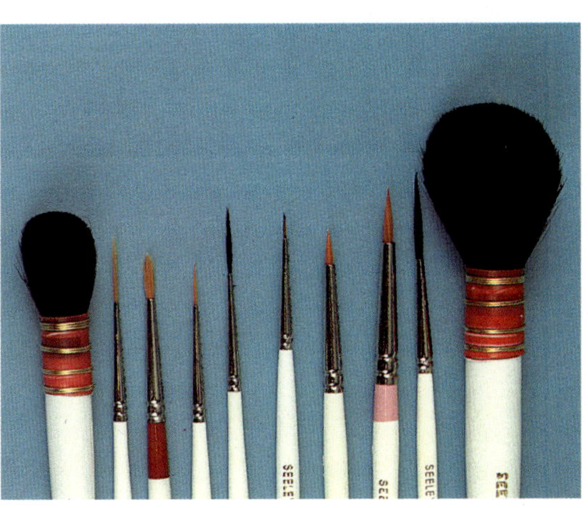

L to R: China Mop #5, Eyebrow Liner #2, Medium Area Brush, Eyelash Liner #1, Eyebrow Brush #1, Accent Liner, Lip Brush #1, Large Area Brush, Super Brow, China Mop #8

There are three synthetic brushes available for painting lips and other areas such as eyes, hair, socks and shoes on all-bisque dolls, nose and eye dots, and some one-stroke eyebrows. All three are round brushes which keep nice points if they are well cared for. The **Lip Brush** (yellow tip) is a small, round brush, good for very small dolls. A favorite brush of many dollmakers is the **Medium Area Brush** (maroon tip), which is capable of painting beautifully-smooth lips. The **Large Area Brush** (pink tip) is simply a larger version of the Medium Area Brush and is used to paint larger dolls.

Dollmakers also need a few natural animal hair brushes. The brushes described below are made of soft, pliable Kazan squirrel hair, which originates in Russia and is the best squirrel hair available. The brush stroke produced by a brush of squirrel hair will be light, soft, and subtle.

The indispensable **China Mop** is available in several sizes and is made of a mixture of several varieties of squirrel hair. China Mops are necessary to polish out an overall wash and for applying and blending cheek color.

The **Eyebrow Brush #1** (red tip) produces lovely, soft, feathered eyebrows on French dolls such as the Jumeau and Bru dolls and many German Kestners. It also paints lovely, soft, shadow brows and can be used for single-stroke eyebrows.

The **Super Brow Brush** (purple tip) looks formidable to many because of its very long hairs. When wet, this unruly looking brush comes to a beautiful point and holds a lot of paint for the softly-colored eyebrows on larger French dolls.

The **Accent Liner** (orange tip), another brush made of Kazan squirrel hair is used, as its name implies, for *lip* accents. Try it also for lid crease lines on painted-eye dolls, tiny one-stroke eyebrows, and detailing, such as the garters on Parian dolls.

Seeley's Doll Pouncer is designed for polishing and applying overall wash and blush. It is sized for use with Blush Pacs.

A number of brushes have been specially developed for the Modern doll artist (they have short red handles). The **Modern Lip Brush** is a small, round brush, excellent for lips and nose and eye dots. The **Angular Shader** is a nice brush to smooth lip color, blend eye shadow, and do eye shading on painted-eye dolls. The **18/0 Mini Liner** is a tiny liner for the smallest eyelashes and eyebrows. Two more very helpful brushes are the **Medium** and **Large Filbert Blenders.** These are indispensable for shading contours on bodies and blending out eye shadow.

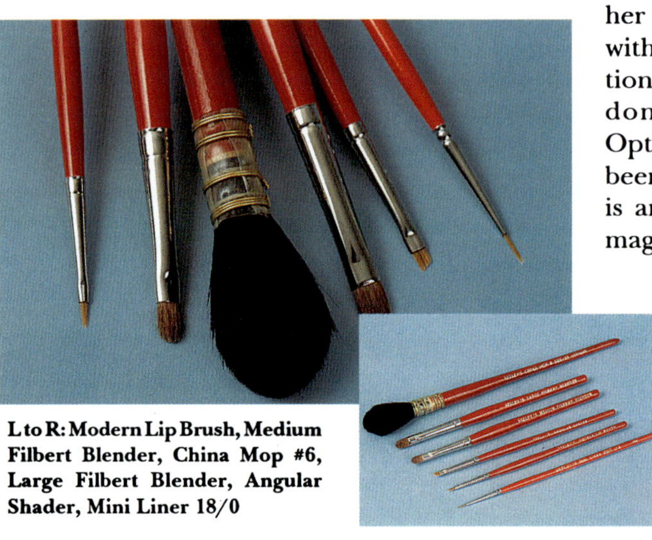

L to R: Modern Lip Brush, Medium Filbert Blender, China Mop #6, Large Filbert Blender, Angular Shader, Mini Liner 18/0

Brush Technique and Practice Makes Perfect

Wish I had a quarter for every time a student said to me "I want one of those trained brushes!" While I must admit that some brushes seem to improve with use, I must say that you, the dollmaker, must be trained, not the brush! Some of the expertise you are striving for is proper technique; the rest is practice, practice, practice!

Brush technique sounds scary. Let's just get to know the brush and how to handle it. First off, to paint well, you must be able to see well and be comfortable. I have met many a student who was getting nowhere in spite of good technique and lots of practice until she put aside her vanity and tried painting with the help of magnification. Even if you think you don't need help, try an Optivisor and see what you've been missing. The Optivisor is an optical glass binocular magnifier on an adjustable headband that makes your painting so much easier.

Adequate lighting and a comfortable table and chair are also essential for good work. For a work surface, I use several thicknesses of a folded old bath towel. This cushions the head I'm working on and gives me a perfect place to wipe my brushes as I work.

Back to the brushes. With the exception of the China Mops, always dip the brush in water before using. Shake or blot out the excess moisture. Brushes are meant to be fully loaded with paint. I see so many students carefully dip only the tip of the brush into the paint. We want to learn to paint with the entire brush; therefore, we must learn to fully load the brush. In the case of liners, either pull the brush hairs through the mixed china paint or roll the hairs in the china paint until the brush is loaded. Now, roll the brush, and pull the brush through the paint and onto the tile. Try a few strokes on the tile. For consistent color, you will need to pull the brush through the mixed color for each stroke. Develop a load-stroke-load-stroke rhythm. Painting with a liner brush is not difficult if you relax and use the brush as it was intended to be used. So many students take a beautiful, long liner and paint with only the tip. What a waste of a wonderful brush! **Lay the brush down.** The entire length of the brush hair should make contact with the porcelain. The more pressure you exert on the brush, the heavier the line.

Occasionally I see someone using a mop brush as if it were a floor mop being used to scrub the kitchen floor! Pinch the hairs together, and hold the mop brush just below the ferrule. This makes a firmer brush. Now use a gentle polishing action to polish out an overall wash or to apply Cheek Blush.

Like all liners, the round brushes must also be loaded fully if they are to do the job they were intended to do. This includes the Lip Brush and the Medium and Large Area Brushes. Roll the brush in the paint to fully load; then pull out a few strokes on the tile to get rid of excess paint. When painting lips, use a large enough brush to paint with as few strokes as possible. Many small, overlapping brush strokes will result in blotchy lip color. This also pertains to eyes, shoes, hair, and other areas of solid color. The fewer the strokes, the better.

Proper brush technique is very important. There are ways to hold the brush and pull strokes that can not be easily conveyed in writing. Please do seek out a Doll Artisan Guild seminar, and have a qualified D.A.G. Instructor demonstrate proper brush technique. Thereafter, the rest is up to you. Serious dollmakers find time to practice what they have learned in the classroom. Keep a practice head handy, and use it often to improve your painting skills. **Practice does make perfect!**

Brush Care and Maintenance

Take care of your brushes, and they will perform well for you. Waterbase china paint washes out of brushes easily with clear water. Occasionally, you may need to clean your brushes more thoroughly by gently washing them in warm water with a mild detergent. Rinse them well with clear water, and allow them to dry naturally.

Never allow your brushes to soak standing in a container of water. The hairs are sure to bend out of shape and will, unfortunately, retain that shape. Gently swish brushes through a container of water, or rinse under running water. Be especially gentle with brushes made of natural animal hair; wiping them on a towel to dry them may damage the delicate hair. These brushes should be blotted dry on a lint-free towel. When not in use, brushes should be stored in an upright container, handle down, to keep brush hair from bending out of shape. A worthwhile investment to protect your good brushes is the handy **Brush Traveler.** The hinged base folds up to allow brushes to

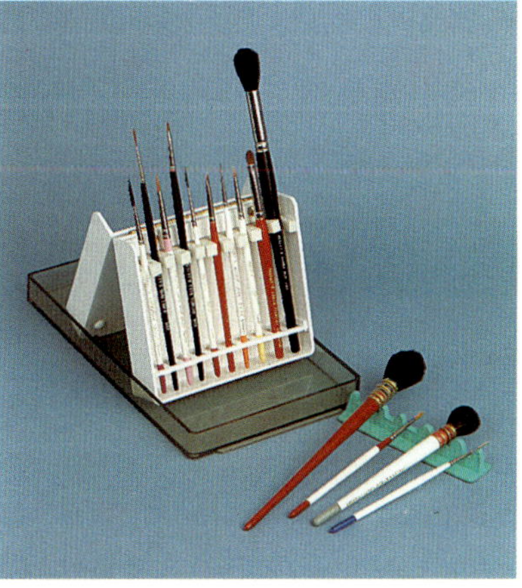

stand for easy access, yet compartments keep them separated. A hard plastic lid snaps on for traveling.

Some dollmakers are using the same hair conditioner used on their hair to condition china mops and other natural hair brushes. The conditioner makes the hair less brittle and less likely to break off. Gently wash brushes with a mild detergent, rinse well, soak brush hair from three to five minutes in a very gentle hair conditioner, rinse out, shape, and allow to dry naturally. After conditioning and rinsing China Mops, twirl the brush handle back and forth between your palms. This rotating motion again fluffs up the mop hair.

8 Bisque Preparation and China Painting

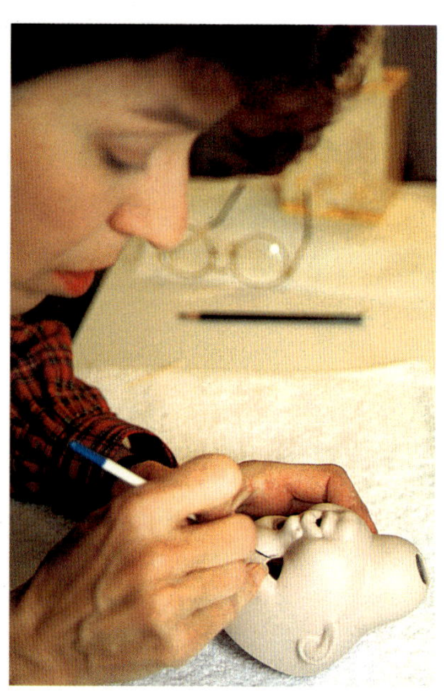

AFTER THE BISQUE FIRE, the porcelain will have a rather rough texture. If china paint is applied to rough bisque, the rough areas will hold the color unevenly, and your doll will have a very blotchy complexion. To prepare the bisque for china painting, sand it lightly with a #220 Grit Scrubber or Seeley's Bisque Sander. Make sure you get in all hard-to-reach places such as nostrils and mouths. Rinse off all grit, and allow the head to air dry completely before china painting. Do not hand dry heads with a cloth or paper towel, as these will put lint on the head, which will interfere with the china painting. Before you begin, wash your hands; body oils or hand cream can "seal" the bisque so it will not accept china paint.

Application of the Overall Wash

Most antique dolls were made of white porcelain. Therefore, for an authentic reproduction, it is preferable to pour the head in one of Seeley's white porcelain slips and use an overall wash of china paint (usually one of the Bisq-Tone colors) to achieve the flesh-tone coloring.

First, rub a thin film of Area Medium over the entire head with your hands or a dry Super Doll Sponge. With the proper amount of medium, the head will have a **slight** sheen; it will not be wet looking. Remove any excess with a dry Super Doll Sponge. Grind the china paint color with Area Medium on a clean,

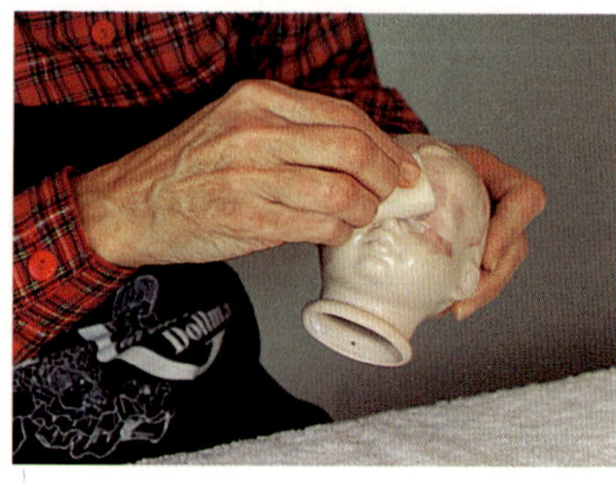

glazed tile to a creamy consistency. Use a clean, dry Super Doll Sponge to apply the overall wash color to the head in long, light strokes.

Grasp the China Mop just **below** the ferrule to hold the hairs together for a firmer brush. Begin with the recessed areas of the eyes,

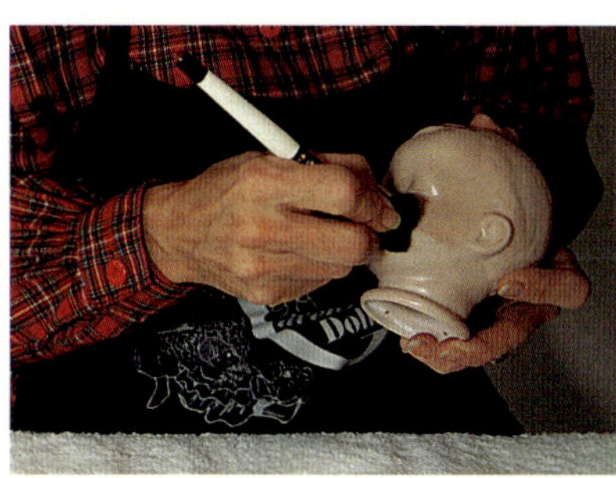

nose, mouth, and ears, and use a stippling/polishing motion to smooth the wash color. As the China Mop becomes saturated with paint and medium, wipe it off on a lint-free towel. Continue to polish the head **quickly** until the color is smooth. Develop a pattern when

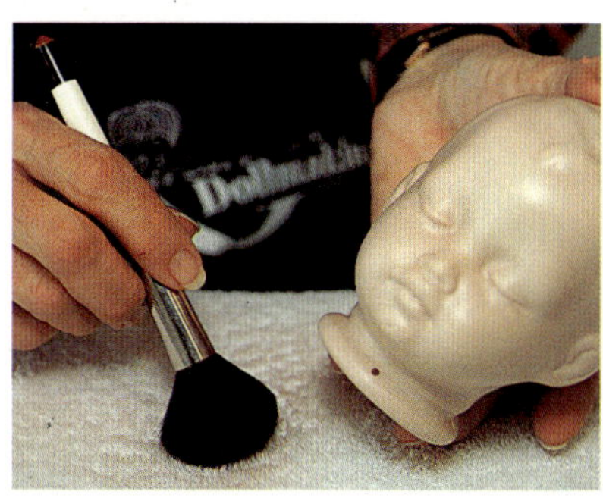

polishing heads, and use it consistently. In other words, complete the eye area before going on to the nose area, and complete it before going on to the mouth area, etc.

You can overwork any china paint, and you'll know you have when the color appears blotchy and chalky and no longer polishes evenly. What has happened is the medium has dried off. To remedy this, simply reapply Area Medium and start anew.

When you have polished the wash color smooth to your satisfaction, you will need to remove the color from any areas which should remain white (teeth, eyes on painted-eye dolls, socks on all-bisque dolls). Use a dampened Medium Area Brush for this purpose. The overall wash is always fired on before any further painting proceeds.

Painting Eyes

Painted-eye dolls have an appeal all their own. Painting the eye gives the doll a unique look that glass eyes cannot duplicate. The demure *K★R 101 Marie* included in this book is an excellent exercise in painting eyes.

Always refer to the worksheet or another good photo reference for the painted-eye doll you are working on to observe the eyes. Which way are they looking? How large is the iris . . . the pupil? Is there a highlight? All of these things are important if you wish to paint beautiful eyes.

Some painted-eye dolls (Heubach's *7620 Robert* and *7851 Singing Susanna)* have **intaglio eyes,** which means the pupil and part of the iris is recessed. This makes placement a little easier. Other painted-eye dolls have a smooth eye surface, and you must decide the position and size of the iris (with the help of the reference photo).

In *Marie's* case, her eyes are looking straight ahead, but the heavy lid line makes her appear to be looking down.

Eyes must be painted in several steps with firing in between. First, mix the blue china paint for the iris as per the worksheet on *Marie* (pages 40-41). You will note that there is a fraction of a drop of Anti-Blotch added to the mixed color to minimize blotching.

Use a water-moistened Me-

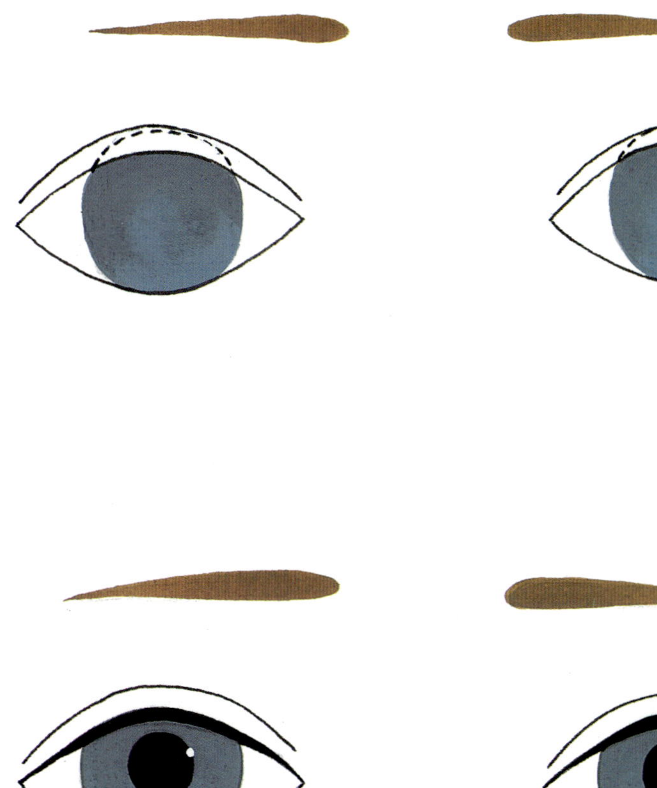

dium Area Brush to paint both the iris and pupil area blue. Note that the iris is not a completely-round circle because the upper part of the iris is under the eyelid. The bottom of the iris rests on the bottom edge of the eye opening.

Always look closely at your reference photo - *Marie* has darker shading along the top of the iris. Add a few grains of black to the blue color, and use this to shade the darker area. Blend the darker area (top of the iris) into the lighter area (bottom half of iris) subtly.

Fire the head before doing further eye work.

Next, mix the black paint as instructed on the worksheet, and use a water-moistened Accent Liner to paint the fairly-heavy lid line. Paint the medium-size round pupils with the Medium Area Brush using the same Black paint used for the lid line. If additional iris shading is needed, add it now, being very careful of the wet pupil.

Small *K★R 101s* did not have a highlight in the eye. If you do wish to paint one, the wet eyes must first be dried off. To do so, place the head in a warm conventional oven or kiln (lid open). The china paint will appear chalky when the medium has dried off. Let the head cool. Be very careful; the paint can still be smudged easily. Dip a toothpick into mixed Satin White, and "dot" the highlight onto the pupil at the two o'clock position. Note that the highlight is always at the same location in **both** eyes.

Fire the head as per the worksheet.

I have been successful at painting Satin White directly on top of wet Onyx Black without drying it off and have had a beautiful highlight after firing.

You will want to try some other painted-eye dolls. *Johann, Ingrid, Lorie,* and *Elise* are just a few examples of other wonderful painted-eye character dolls.

Lashes

The most frequent problems encountered while painting lashes involve inconsistencies in length and color intensity. To get lashes of consistent length every time, mark the length on the bisque head with a series of pencil dots, which will fire off during the china fire. Color intensity will be consistent if the brush is reloaded for each lash stroke. China paint for lashes should be mixed to a light, creamy consistency. Paint lashes with a trimmed Eyelash Liner #1. Always check photo references for position and length.

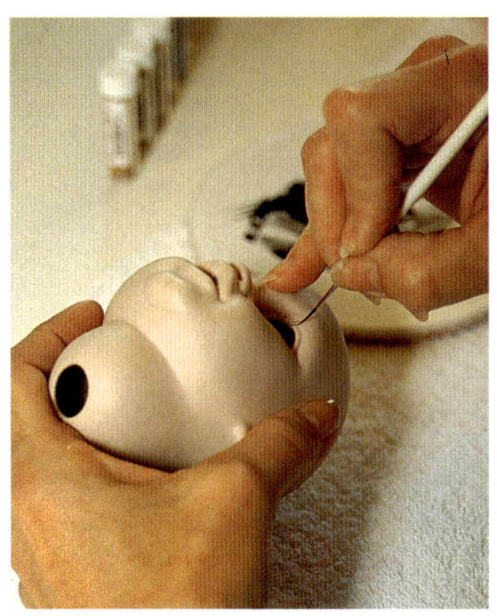

Support the head in a comfortable position **on the table . . .** not with your lap. Turn the head upside down, and beginning with the top lashes, paint the lashes from the inner corner of the eye to the outer corner. Turn the head, and paint the bottom lashes from the inner corner to the outer corner. Some dolls have a painted eye rim either on the top only or around the entire eye cut. Paint the eye rim with the Eyelash Liner by rubbing the hair at the base of the ferrule along the rim edge.

What if you make a mistake and wish to remove one or two lashes? Either clean off the bad lash(es) with a dampened Medium Area Brush, or use a piece of Dolly Dough.

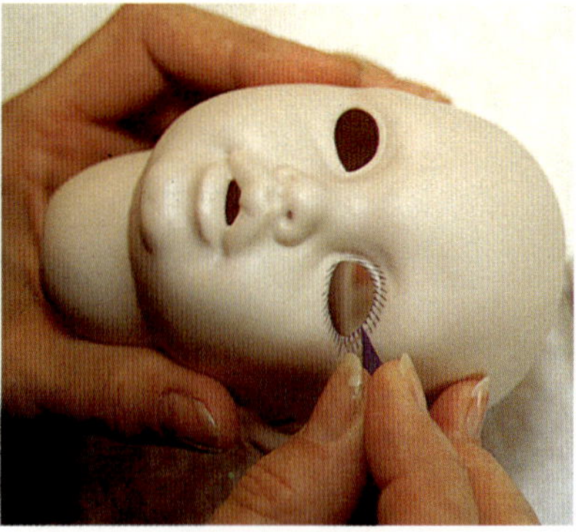

Remove a bad lash with Dolly Dough.

Lips, Nose and Eye Dots

Mix china paint for lips, nose and eye dots to a heavy-cream consistency, and add a fraction of a drop of Anti-Blotch. Never attempt to paint lips by outlining and filling in the shape. The result will be blotchy lips. Instead, use the Medium Area Brush, well loaded, to paint the lips in as few strokes as possible. Painting smooth lips requires practice. In time, this will become second nature, but until that day, you may use a dry, Square Shader to eliminate

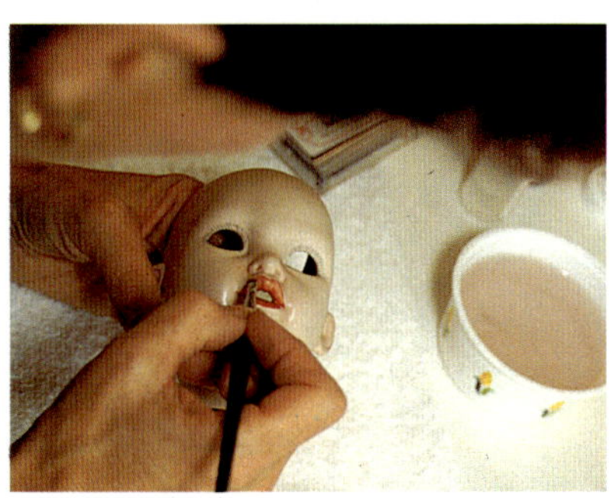

brush lines and uneven areas. A word of caution about using Anti-Blotch. While Anti-Blotch does help minimize blotchiness, its addition will cause the china paint to dry off faster, and an invisible skin will form. Therefore, if blotting lips or using a brush to smooth lips, work very fast or eliminate the use of Anti-Blotch.

Nose and eye dots are generally kept light and are also painted with the Medium Area Brush.

Eyebrows

Eyebrows can range from subdued, fuzzy baby eyebrows such as *Averill Baby's,* to the simple one-stroke eyebrows of our *K★R 101 Marie,* to the beautifully-feathered eyebrows of a Jumeau. Whether painting a simple or intricate eyebrow, correct and symmetrical placement will be easier if you mark the brow position with light pencil dots. No need to worry about covering the pencil marks, as they will fire off.

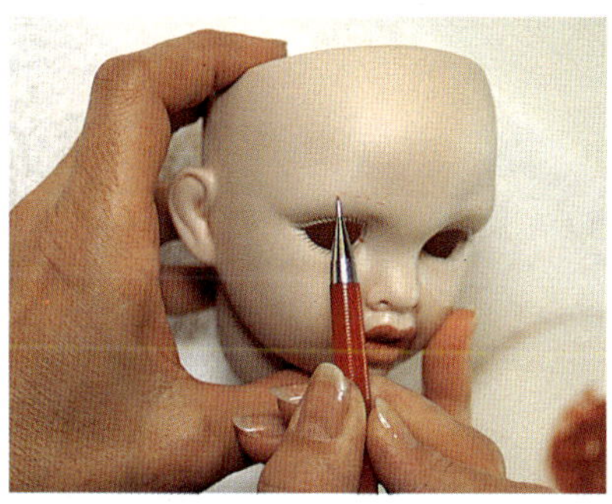

Eyebrow placement will be easier if you pencil mark the brow position before painting.

A simple baby eyebrow is created using a water-moistened Medium Area Brush and china paint mixed with Line Medium to a rather runny consistency. Paint the eyebrows in one stroke; then use a Small Square Shader to lightly diffuse all edges, leaving a soft, fuzzy eyebrow.

Many eyebrows are painted in two firings. The first, the underbrow

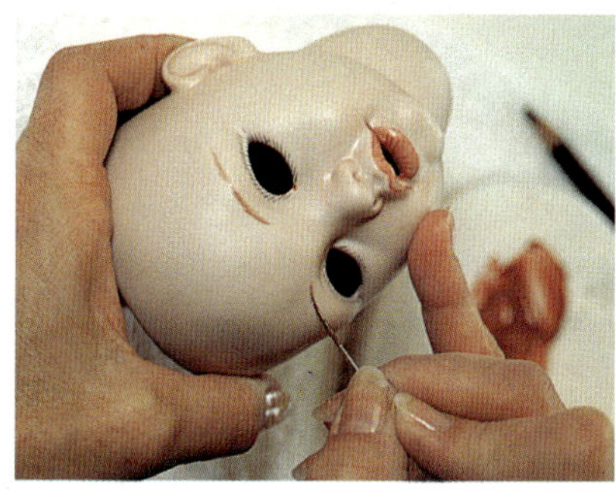

or shadow brow, should be a light, smooth stroke painted with a water-moistened Medium Area Brush. On the second firing, feathered lines are added with one of the eyebrow brushes to cover the underbrow. China paint for feathered brows is mixed to a light, creamy consistency, and depending on the type of lines one wants, the brush used would be Eyebrow Brush #1, Eyebrow Liner #2, or the Super Brow Brush. For a description of each of these brushes, refer to the chapter on brushes.

Painted Hair

Many babies (such as *Baby Chrissy,* pages 38-39) have painted hair rather than wigs. Well-executed painted hair has darker color on the crown area of the head, fading to the hairline so that there is no harsh line of demarcation where the hairline and the complexion meet. The most popular color for babies is Russet.

To paint baby hair, first rub a small amount of Area Medium all over the hair area and down a bit below the hairline. Mix china paint color to a dense consistency, and apply it with a Super Doll Sponge. Beginning at the crown, use a stippling action to even out the color

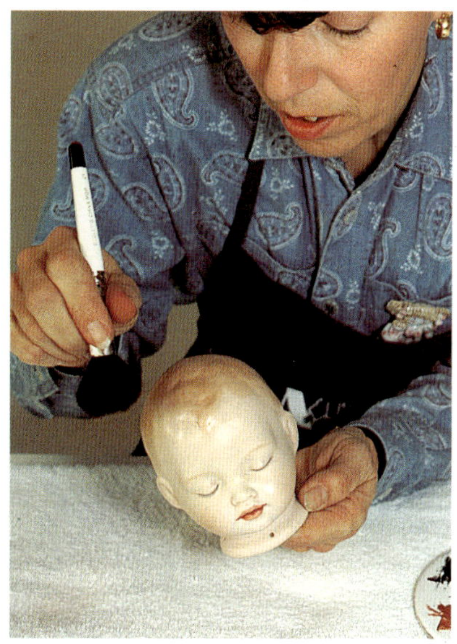

Use a China Mop to lightly smooth away any uneven marks.

smoothly, working to eliminate any hint of a line at the hairline. Next, use a China Mop to lightly work out any marks left by the sponge. I strongly recommend a separate China Mop, marked and kept exclusively for hair color.

Some reproduction dolls such as *Whistler, Elsbeth,* and the dome head *Hilda* have hair that appears to be stroked on. To apply this type of hair, the color may be stroked on with a water-moistened Fan Brush or streaked on with a coarse sponge. In either case, stroke or streak the hair color on from crown to hairline, lightening color at hairline.

Cheek Blush

Cheek Blush color is available in either dry powder form, which must be mixed, or in a convenient pre-mixed Cheek Blush Pac in a choice of two colors. Cheek Blush is a lovely, deep red-rose color. Ruby Cheek Blush is a stronger cheek color for dolls with "apple" cheeks.

If you prefer to use dry cheek blush colors, they must be mixed to a firm "Cheek Blush Cake" before using. To mix a Cheek Blush Cake, mix one vial of Cheek Blush with Line Medium to a stiff paste consistency. Add another vial of china paint and just enough water to create a smooth paste. Spread this paste in a small, flat container. Place this container of Cheek Blush in a warm, dry place until the water evaporates. Placing the freshly-made Cheek Blush Cake in front of a dehumidifier will speed up the process of evaporating the water. A properly-made Cheek Blush Cake will be quite firm - the consistency of shoe polish. A Cheek Blush Cake will keep indefinitely. If it becomes too wet, blot off the excess moisture; if too dry, rub a drop or two of Line Medium over the surface. The Cheek Blush Cake should be kept clean and covered when not in use.

To apply Cheek Blush, first rub a **thin** film of Area Medium over the area to be blushed. Hold the China Mop, pinching the brush hair together just below the ferrule. Rub the hairs of the China Mop firmly over the Cheek Blush Cake, and

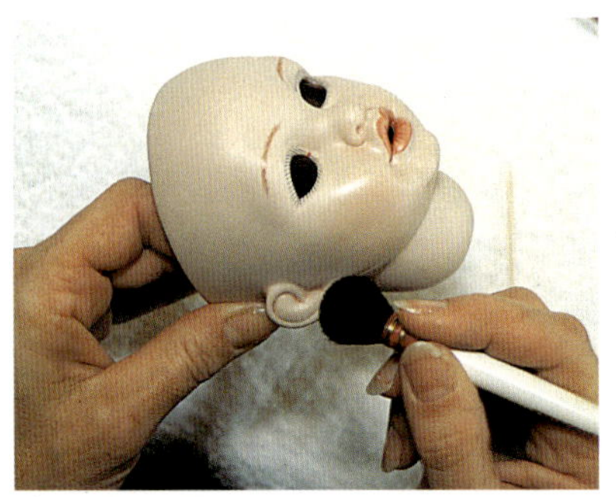

apply the color to the cheeks, blending and fading out the color around the edges. Don't overdo the amount of color on the first firing. More color can always be added on a subsequent firing.

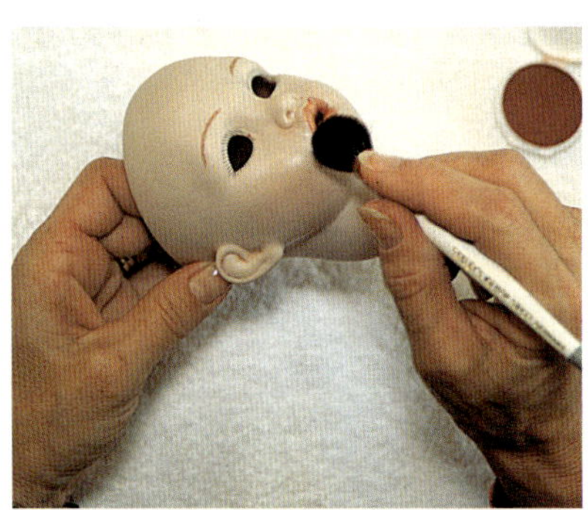

Inspect your china painting as you work to ensure that your painting is well balanced.

Chrissy

Precious, slumbering *Chrissy* with her serene, beautifully-sculpted face is a baby doll on a wonderful poseable cloth body. Her full lips turn up with just a hint of a smile, making you wonder what sweet baby dreams she is dreaming. *Chrissy* has painted hair but could be made with a sparse, wispy baby wig. This doll is a joy to behold and great fun to paint. *Chrissy* looks adorable in a little flannel sleeper.

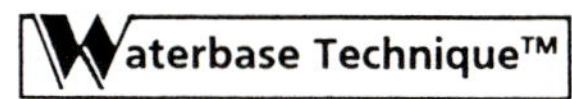

S872 Chrissy

Repro size: 17" (43cm)
S872 *Chrissy*© head mold
A9872 hand mold
Body: BP70 Cloth, filled with Baby Beans (see page 48)
Head circ.: 11.5" (29cm)
Pattern:
MP41 Sleeper with variations

Porcelain slip: French Chocolate™

China Painting Supplies

- China Paints
  - Mocha
  - Satin Black
  - Ruby Cheek Blush
  - Rose Red
  - Yellow-Red
- Line Medium
- Area Medium
- Anti-Blotch
- China Mop #8
- China Mop #5
- Medium Filbert Blender
- Medium Area Brush
- Eyelash Liner #1
- Eyebrow Brush #1
- Accent Liner
- Small Square Shader
- Super Doll Sponges™
- Orton Junior cones 017, 018
- Orton witness cones 018, 019

Optional China Paint Colors for White *Chrissy*

Porcelain: Seeley's French Bisque®

First Firing:

Facial Contours and Hands: Ruby Cheek Blush
Eye Lids: Light Blue
Lips & Nose Dots: Equal parts Rose Red and Pompadour Red
Cheeks and Backs of Hands: Ruby Cheek Blush

Second Firing:

Eyelashes: Satin Black
Eyebrows and Hair: Russet
Lip Shading & Accents: Equal parts Rose Red and Pompadour Red Gloss
Cheeks: Same as above

PAINTING SCHEDULE

First Firing: Orton Junior cone 017 in sitter, witness cone 018 on shelf.

1. OVERALL WASH
Mocha
Area Medium
Super Doll Sponge
China Mop #8 (Black)

Mix paint with Area Medium to a loose but creamy consistency. Color: deep green-brown. Apply evenly to the head with a Doll Sponge. Lightly polish with a China Mop, first stippling into the detailed areas.

Second Firing: Orton Junior cone 017 in sitter, witness cone 018 on shelf.

1. FACIAL CONTOURS & HANDS
Ruby Cheek Blush
Area Medium
Super Doll Sponge
Medium Area Brush (Maroon)
Medium Filbert Blender

Apply thin film of Area Medium to all recessed areas of face and hands (sides of nose, dimple, eyelid crease, etc.). Mix china paint to creamy consistency. Use Medium Area Brush to apply color to all creases. Blend color out naturally with Medium Filbert Blender. Apply color lightly to fingernails with Medium Area Brush.

2. LIPS, NOSE DOTS
1 part Rose Red
1 part Yellow-Red
Line Medium
Medium Area Brush (Maroon)

Paint consistency: Creamy. Color: Light. Paint light, smooth coat of color on lips.

3. EYELASHES & EYEBROWS
Satin Black
Line Medium
Eyelash Liner #1 (Blue), trimmed
Eyebrow Brush #1 (Red)
Water

Mix paint to a light, creamy consistency. Add drop of water to thin paint. Use Eyelash Liner #1 to paint lid line and lashes. Paint individual eyebrow hairs with Eyebrow Brush.

4. HAIR
Satin Black
Area Medium
Super Doll Sponge
China Mop #5 (Gray)

Apply thin film of Area Medium to hair area of head. Use a Doll Sponge to pounce on hair color, blending subtly around hairline. Use China Mop reserved for hair color to polish color smooth.

5. CHEEKS
1 part Yellow-Red
1 part Ruby Cheek Blush
Area Medium
China Mop #5 (Gray)

Apply Area Medium sparingly. Use China Mop #5 to apply nice rosy baby cheeks. Blend color from outer edges into center with no apparent stop/start line.

Third Firing: Orton Junior cone 018 in sitter, witness cone 019 on shelf.

1. LIP SHADING & ACCENTS
1 part Yellow Red
1 part Ruby Cheek Blush
Medium Area Brush (Maroon)
Small Square Shader
Accent Liner (Orange)

Paint another coat of color in center lip crease. Use Small Square Shader to blend color outward, but keep color wet in crease. Use Accent Liner to add lip accents.

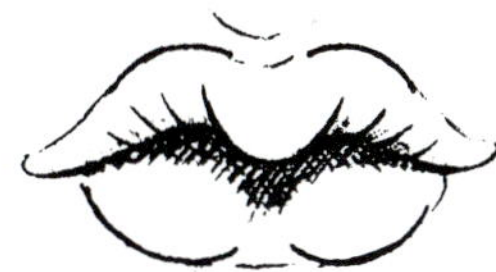

2. CHEEKS
Same color as Cheeks, Second Firing

Add additional color, if necessary.

Antique doll from private collection

Brown Version

Antique *K★R 101* was produced with either painted or glass eyes.

Antique doll courtesy Rosemary Post

K★R Peter and Marie

The superbly modeled mold number *101 Peter/Marie* is a portrait of a wistful child created by Kämmer & Reinhardt in 1909. Mold #101, one of Kämmer & Reinhardt's first character models, was made as a girl or boy, in sizes from 9" to 20". Rare versions of this doll have glass eyes, and brown bisque models with dark brown painted eyes were also produced.

Shy *Marie* would be lovely in a mohair wig with a center part and either long braids or braids tightly coiled at each ear. A short, cropped wig would be a suitable style for *Peter*.

Peter would look handsome in a lightweight sailor suit; while *Marie* would be appropriately attired in a simple white dress with a frill around the yoke or a provincial costume.

Photos of Antique *K★R101 Peter/Marie*

The Doll as Art, Stuart Holbrook, Theriault's Gold Horse Publishing, p. 104 (excellent)

Rare Character Dolls, Maree Tarnowska, Hobby House Press 1987, p. 81

Brown Bisque Version

Simon & Halbig Dolls, Jan Foulke, Hobby House Press 1984, p. 23

German Children Dolls, Mildred Seeley, Scott Publications 1990, p. 46

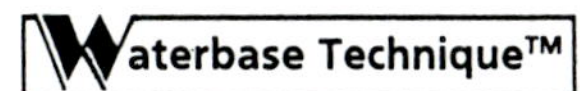

K★R 101
Peter and Marie

Repro size: 10" (25cm)
S56 *Peter*© head mold
Compo body: GB7
Body mold: ALB9201
Head circ.: 6.5" (16.5cm)
Patterns:
CP211 Regional costume for boy and girl

Repro size: 9" (23cm)
S6 *K★R 101*© head mold
Compo body: GB6
Body mold: ALB9412
Head circ.: 5.75" (14.5cm)
Patterns:
CP9002 Regional costume for girl
CP9001 Dress, hat, apron, underwear

Porcelain slip: Lady White™ or Nordic White™

China Painting Supplies

- China Paints
  - Bisq-Tone #2 Raspberry
  - Teal Blue
  - Onyx Black
  - Yellow-Red
  - Pompadour Red
  - Eyebrow #4D Dark, dark-brown
  - Ruby Cheek Blush Pac
  - Satin White
- Line Medium
- Area Medium
- Anti-Blotch
- Medium Area Brush
- Accent Liner
- China Mop #8
- China Mop #5
- Lip Brush #1 (optional)
- Super Doll Sponges™

PAINTING SCHEDULE

First Firing: Orton Junior cone 017 in sitter, Orton witness cone 018 on shelf.

1. OVERALL WASH
Bisq-Tone #2
Area Medium
Super Doll Sponges
China Mop #8 (Black)
Paint consistency: Creamy. Color: Medium Bluish-rose. Remove color from eye area with a dampened Medium Area Brush.

Second Firing: Orton Junior cone 018 in sitter, Orton witness cone 019 on shelf.

1. IRIS
Teal Blue
Few grains Onyx Black
Line Medium
Anti-Blotch
Medium Area Brush (Maroon)
Mix paint with Line Medium, adding a fraction of a drop of Anti-Blotch. Paint consistency: Creamy. Paint smooth iris and pupil area, shading darker along upper part of iris.

2. LIPS, NOSE DOTS
Yellow-Red
Pompadour Red
Line Medium
Anti-Blotch
Medium Area Brush (Maroon)
Paint consistency: Creamy. Paint light, smooth coat of color.

3. CHEEKS
Ruby Cheek Blush Pac
Area Medium
China Mop #5 (Gray)
Rub light film of Area Medium over cheeks. Apply color to fat part of cheeks.

Third Firing: Orton Junior cone 017 in sitter, Orton witness cone 018 on shelf.

1. PUPILS, LID LINE
Onyx Black
Line Medium
Medium Area Brush (Maroon)
Accent Liner (Orange)
Paint consistency: Creamy. Paint pupil with Medium Area Brush. Paint heavy lid line with water-moistened Accent Liner (for lighter color).

2. IRIS SHADING
Same color as Iris above
Medium Area Brush (Maroon)
Add extra shading to top of iris, if necessary.

3. EYEBROWS
Eyebrow #4D
Medium Area Brush (Maroon) or Lip Brush #1 (Yellow)
Line Medium
Anti-Blotch
Paint consistency: Light. Color: Translucent brown. Paint with water-moistened Medium Area Brush or Lip Brush.

4. LIPS
1 part Yellow-Red
1 part Pompadour Red
Line Medium
Medium Area Brush (Maroon)
Add accent line through center of mouth. Blend out toward edges of lips.

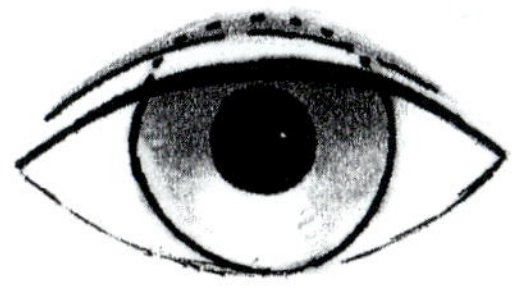

5. CHEEKS
Ruby Cheek Blush Pac
Area Medium
China Mop #5 (Gray)
Add extra color to cheeks, if necessary.

OPTIONAL: The *K★R 101* dolls under 18" in height did not have highlights in the eyes. However, you may prefer this extra sparkle. If you wish to highlight eyes, place the head in a warm kiln (low setting) or oven (around 250° F.) until medium dries off. Continue with #6.

6. HIGHLIGHT (Optional)
Satin White
Line Medium
Round toothpick
Paint consistency: Heavy cream. "Dot" on highlight with tip of toothpick at the two o'clock position.

BROWN VARIATION
Pour doll in French Chocolate or Aztec Tan porcelain slip.
Mouth, nose dots, and cheeks: Persian Red (Flesh)
Iris: 1 part Eyebrow #3D Dark Copper to 1 part Eyebrow #4D plus a few grains Onyx Black.
Pupils, Lid Line, Eyebrows: Onyx Black

Angel

Angel - what a perfect name for this charming and innocent young miss. Her large, engaging eyes and sweet smile are sure to steal your heart. *Angel's* beautifully-sculpted, very special little girl body is too pretty to cover up. It is the perfect body to dress in a pinafore or sun suit.

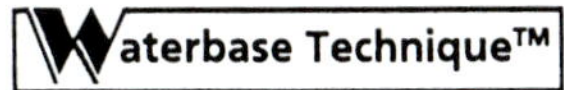

S873 Angel

Repro size: 18" (46cm)
S873 *Angel*© head mold
Body mold: ALB9873
Eye size: 16mm paperweight (PW16BR/BL)
Head circ.: 10.25" (26cm)
Patterns:
CP931 Summer dress and underwear

Porcelain slip: Aztec Tan™

China Painting Supplies

- China Paints
  - Mahogany
  - Onyx Black
  - Black Matt
  - Ruby Cheek Blush Pac
  - Ruby Cheek Blush
- Line Medium
- Area Medium
- Medium Area Brush
- Accent Liner
- Anti-Blotch
- Small Square Shader
- China Mop #5
- China Mop #8
- Eyelash Liner #1
- Eyebrow Liner #2
- Medium Area Brush
- Super Doll Sponges™

Optional China Paint Colors for French Bisque *Angel*
Porcelain: Seeley's French Bisque®
China Paints:
Body Shading: 1 part Rose Red, 1 part Pompadour Red Gloss
Lips, Nose and Eye Dots: Same as body shading on 2nd Firing. Shade, and add lip accents with Pompadour Red Gloss
Eyebrows: Eyebrow #1 Dark Toffee
Eyelashes: 1 part Onyx Black to 1 part Black Matt
Cheek Blush: Ruby Cheek Pac

PAINTING SCHEDULE

First Firing: Orton Junior cone 017 in sitter, Orton witness cone 018 on shelf.

1. OVERALL WASH
Mahogany
Super Doll Sponge
Area Medium

Paint consistency: Creamy. Wipe thin application of Area Medium over head and all.body parts. Apply color with sponge and China Mop #8; polish with China Mop. Allow color to remain darker between fingers, toes, and in any creases.

Second Firing: Orton Junior cone 018 in sitter, Orton witness cone 019 on shelf.

1. EYELASHES
1 part Onyx Black
1 part Black Matt
Line Medium
Eyelash Liner #1 (Blue), trimmed

Mix equal parts of Onyx Black and Black Matt. Paint consistency: Creamy, light. Paint fine, angled, irregular bottom lashes.

2. EYEBROWS
Color same as above
Eyebrow Liner #2 (Green)

Use same mixture as used for eyelashes to paint long, delicate eyebrows.

3. LIPS, NOSE & EYE DOTS
Ruby Cheek Blush
Line Medium
Anti-Blotch
Medium Area Brush (Maroon)
Small Square Shader

Paint consistency: Creamy. Paint smooth coat of color on lips with the Medium Area Brush. Use the Small Square Shader to smooth lips, if necessary. Paint small, light nose and eye dots.

4. CHEEKS, BODY BLUSH
Ruby Cheek Blush Pac
Area Medium
China Mop #5 (Gray)

Apply Area Medium to cheek area, and use China Mop to apply color to the cheeks. Repeat blush procedure on elbows, tops of hands, shoulders, outside of thighs, knees, tops of feet, tummy, chest, and buttocks.

Third Firing: Orton Junior cone 018 in sitter, Orton witness cone 019 on shelf.

1. LIPS & NAILS
Ruby Cheek Blush
Line Medium
Small Square Shader
Accent Liner (Orange)

Paint consistency: Creamy. Apply more color around mouth; cut and blend color out subtly. Use the Accent Liner to paint lip highlights and accent lines. Accent fingernails in same manner as the lips.

2. CHEEKS
Ruby Cheek Blush Pac
Area Medium
China Mop #5 (Gray)

Apply more color, if necessary. Give *Angel* nice, rosy cheeks.

9 Choosing and Setting Eyes

I'VE STRESSED BEFORE how very important the doll's eyes are. You've cut out and sized the sockets perfectly; now is the time to choose eyes and fit them. Choosing the proper eyes to bring your treasured doll to life can be quite a chore. After all, there are all types of acrylic eyes, glass eyes, and paperweight eyes in various shades of blue, brown, gray, and green, in round shapes and oval shapes, with different size irises and pupils! How does one choose?

First, is this a contemporary doll or a reproduction doll? We are somewhat limited as to size and type of eyes when doing reproduction dolls. Antique baby dolls most often were made with blue glass eyes, although they are occasionally found with brown or gray eyes. Baby dolls, most German dolly-face dolls, and character dolls very often were made with sleep eyes and occasionally even flirty eyes (eyes that move from side to side and open and close). Most German dolls and some later French dolls have glass eyes in shades of blue, brown, and gray. The French Fashion dolls and bébés and a few German dolls have lovely paperweighted eyes.

Contemporary or imagination dolls are another story. As long as the eye "fits" well, color and type are up to the discretion of the dollmaker.

Fit is so very important. We must consider not only how the eye fits in the eye socket, but also the size of the iris in relation to the eye cut. The iris should not be so large that no white shows nor should it be so small that white is exposed all around it.

When deciding on plastic versus glass eyes, my advice to you would be to purchase the best you can afford. It seems a disservice to the doll to set plastic eyes in her after putting in hours of painstaking "labor" bringing this lovely "being" to life. We all harbor the hope that our dolls will become treasured heirlooms someday. So why not make them with only the best materials.

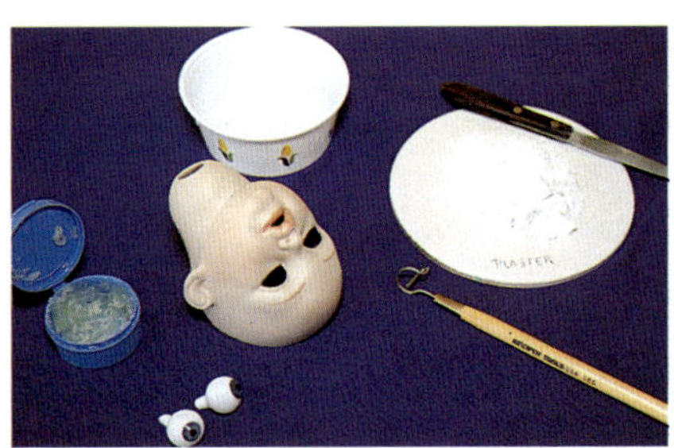

Setting Stationary Eyes

Supplies:

- Suitable eyes
- Eye-setting wax
- Plaster or *Rock Hard*™
- Tile
- Palette Knife
- Water
- ST15 Eye Setting Tool (optional)

We will temporarily set the eyes into the head with eye wax so that both eyes may be adjusted to look in the same direction. Roll a small ball of eye wax into a coil, and either press it around the beveled eye socket **inside** the head or place

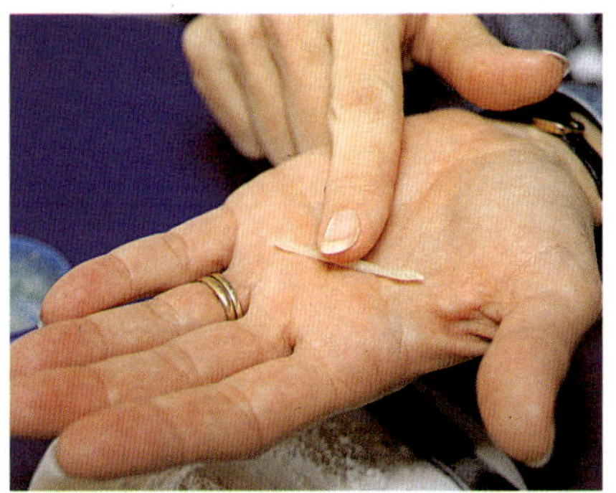

Roll wax into a coil and place it inside on the beveled eye holes.

it on the eye itself, where the eye will contact the bisque. Firmly press the eyes into the sockets, and adjust them so that both eyes focus together.

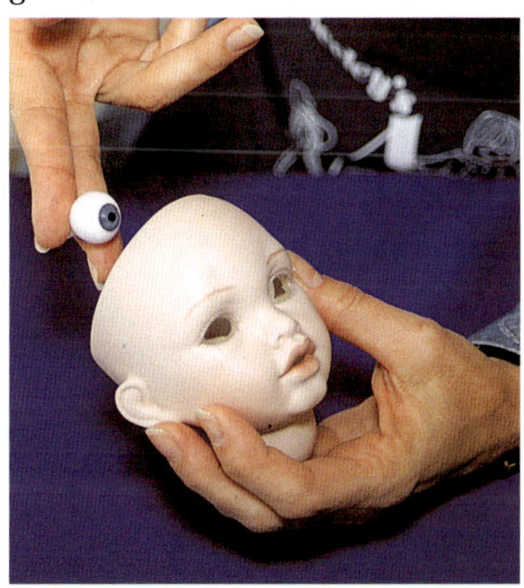

If working on a dome-head doll or another head where your fingers won't quite reach the eye, use an Eye Setting Tool. This tool holds the eye, making it easier for insertion into the head.

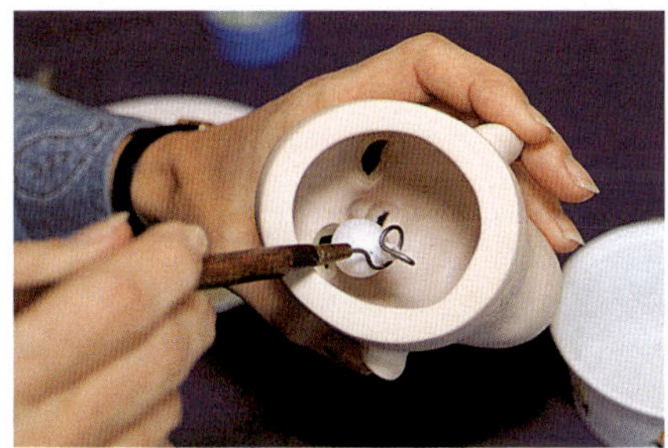

To avoid a staring or startled look when positioning eyes to look straight ahead, position the eye so that the pupil is not dead center but turned up just a bit. Remember the example of the painted eyes; part of the iris is up under the eyelid.

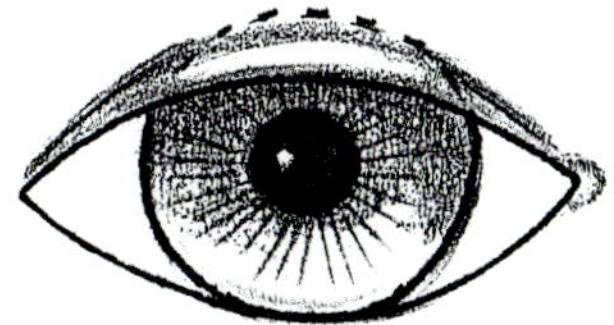

You might prefer eyes glancing to one side or another. That's fine and certainly adds to the character of the doll. Just be sure the eyes are **both** looking in the same direction. Try different eye positions on your contemporary dolls. You will find that it is very easy to change the doll's expression by repositioning her eyes.

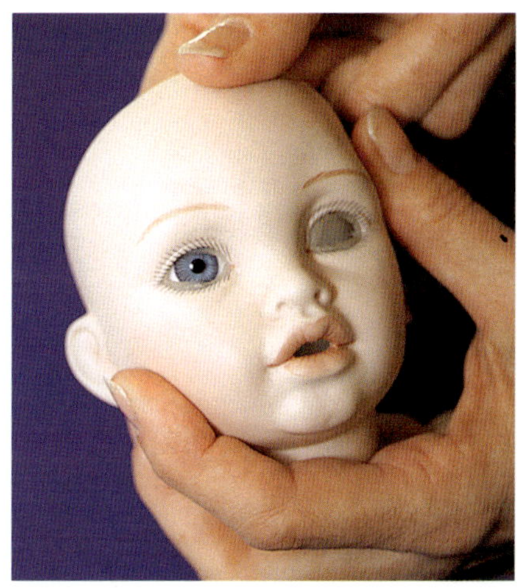

When the eyes are positioned to your liking, lay the head face down on a soft towel. Mix your choice of eye-setting compound

(plaster) with water to a wet but not runny consistency, and use a Palette Knife to place some compound on the sides of the eye and the adjoining bisque surface. Allow the head

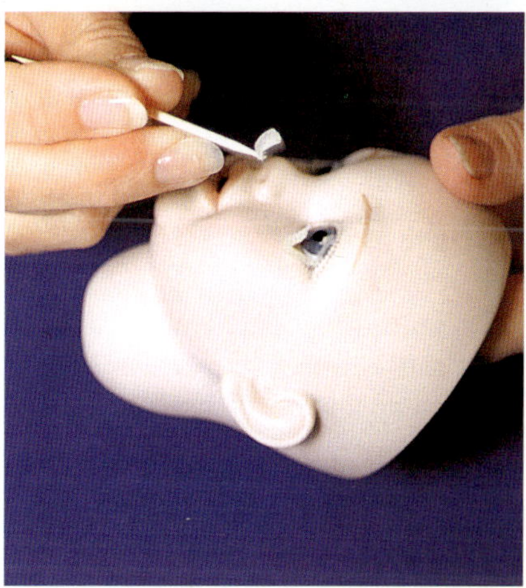

to sit undisturbed until the eye compound is hard. Use a toothpick to remove any wax residue from the eye and the face of the doll. Denatured alcohol cleans up glass eyes beautifully but should not be used on plastic eyes as it can dull some plastics.

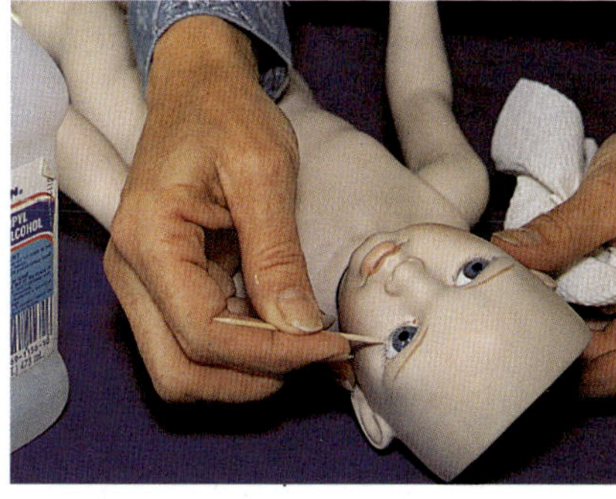

CAUTION: If your doll has an open mouth, be very careful not to allow any eye compound to run out of the mouth opening. Prop the head in such a manner that the plaster, if mixed too runny, will run **away from** the mouth cut.

Other Considerations

Oriental dolls and some French dolls have eye cuts that are difficult to fit with round eyes. These eye cuts usually are better fitted with **oval** eyes.

Teeth

Teeth are set in the same manner as eyes: First with a bit of wax, then with wet but firm eye compound. Compound must be mixed firm to prevent it from running out of the mouth. Do be careful not to give your doll a "Bugs Bunny" look. Choose properly-sized teeth, and set them so that they don't stick out! For more information on setting teeth, refer to Seeley's excellent Dollmaker's Worksheet *WSBDA: Setting Teeth/Tongue.*

Eyelashes

There are some things one must consider when choosing artificial eyelashes. A number of styles of eyelashes are available in different widths, lengths, and thicknesses. Baby innocence would be spoiled by applying too thick or too long lashes. Rather, shorter, sparser lashes would add to the gentle look of an infant. An older child might have fuller lashes, and a doll depicting a mature figure would have fuller and longer lashes still.

The instructions given here are for the application of lashes to a sleeping baby such as *Baby Chrissy* or *My Princess,* or to a doll such as *Angel,* where stationary eyes have already been set.

Materials:
- Eyelashes
- Toothpick
- Glass adhesive

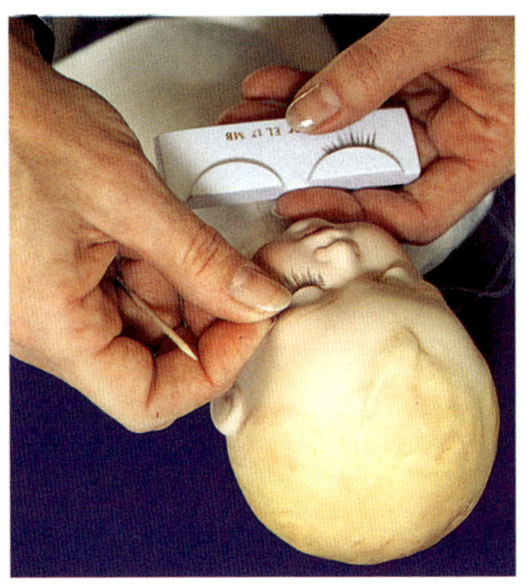

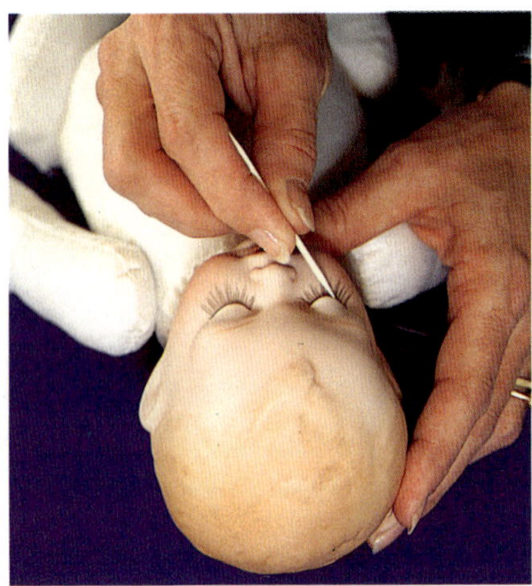

Application

Remove one set of eyelashes from container. Notice, there is a definite left and right. The lashes are always shorter at the inner corner of the eye. On a sleeping baby, place the eyelashes in the lid crease. The sticky substance along the top edge of the eyelashes will hold them in place temporarily. Use a toothpick to position eyelashes properly. After the eyelashes have been positioned to your satisfaction, use a toothpick to dot small droplets of a glass adhesive along the top edge of the lashes.

On open-eyed dolls, place the lashes tightly up against the upper lid. Position with a toothpick, and glue as described above. If any adhesive accidently smears onto the glass eye, clean it off with a denatured alcohol-moistened cotton swab.

10 Body Assembly

HUMAN BODIES come in all shapes and sizes, and so do doll bodies. There are cloth bodies, leather bodies, composition bodies, and porcelain bodies in a multitude of sizes and shapes.

Cloth Bodies

Flange-neck baby dolls are found on cloth bodies of various styles. Reproduction baby dolls generally have simple bodies of cloth, filled with polyester fiber, while contemporary flange-neck babies usually have more poseable bodies filled

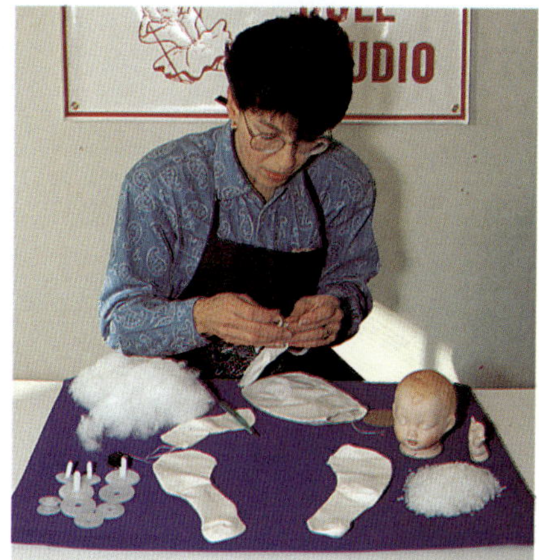

with Baby Beans (plastic pellets) to make them look and feel more lifelike. The body pattern here in Chapter 10 is for our sweet *Baby Chrissy.*

Some other flange-neck, cloth-bodied Baby dolls are the reproduction babies *Tynie Babe, My Dream*

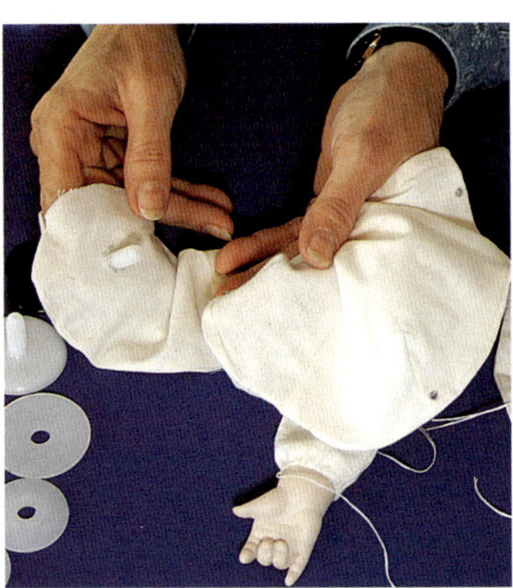

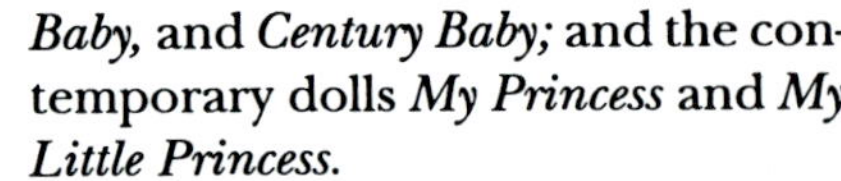

Baby, and *Century Baby;* and the contemporary dolls *My Princess* and *My Little Princess.*

Not only babies are made with cloth bodies. A number of socket-

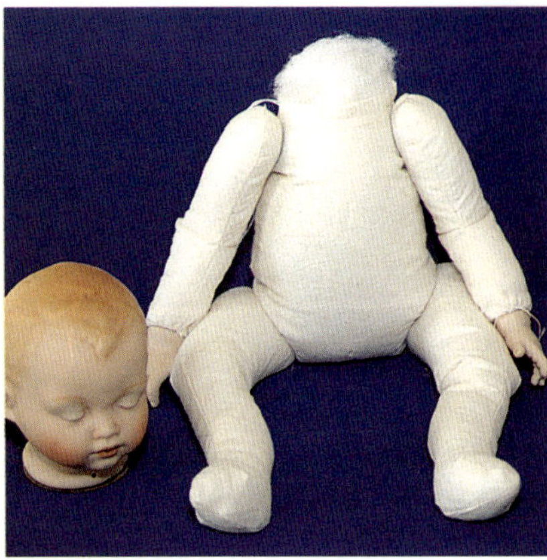

head dolls are put together with a porcelain breast plate and lower arms and legs on a cloth body. The lovely

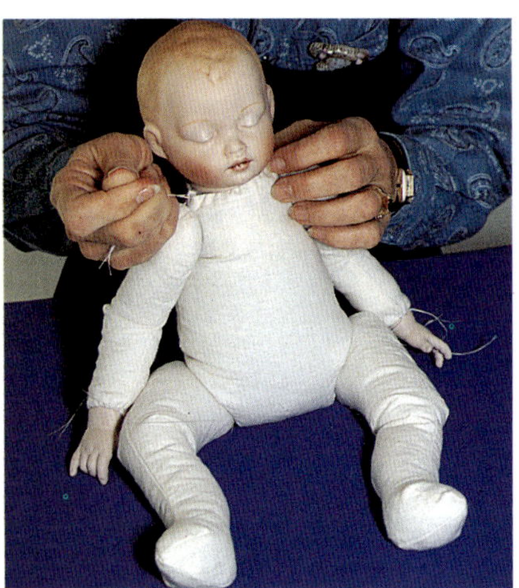

contemporary *Clarissa* is put together in this manner, and a number of reproduction Parian and Lady dolls have cloth bodies with either attached or separate shoulder plates.

Composition Bodies

Composition bodies are marvelously well-made, fully-articulated, and virtually unbreakable bodies. Seeley's offers a selection of 66 different bodies ranging from 6" to 24" (15 to 61cm), in styles suitable for any type doll. There are many bodies for reproduction dolls ranging from fat baby bodies with well-sculpted bellies and chubby, dimpled baby arms and legs, to authentic, fully-jointed French and German bodies, to shapely lady bodies, to very specialized bodies such as the *A. Marque.* There is also a beautiful line of modern bodies with gracefully-sculpted hands and feet.

These bodies are available ei-

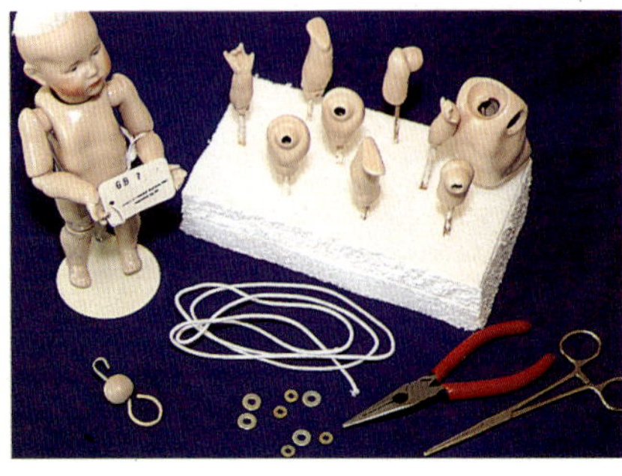

ther strung or unstrung. Strung bodies are painted and assembled, held together with a Body Ball and ready for the doll head to be attached.

Attaching the head to a strung body is a very simple procedure. One merely pulls up on the Body Ball, places something sturdy (a ruler or pair of scissors) under the elastic, unhooks the Body Ball and places it inside the head with the hook extended through the neck opening, and finally attaches the hook of the Body Ball to the body elastic again. Voilá, the doll is created! Nothing could be easier, and you have a durable, beautiful, correct body for your special doll.

Unstrung bodies are sanded but need to be painted and assembled. Special body stains have been formulated to complement Seeley's most popular skin-tone porcelains.

SN1 for Seeley's French Bisque®
SN21 for American Bisque™
SN9 for Oriental Flesh™
SN19 for French Chocolate®
SN6 for Brown Velvet™
SN23 for Aztec Tan™

Also available is Seeley's Nail Stain (SN50) for detailing fingers and toes. These stains, which require no sealer, may be applied to either painted or unpainted composition bodies. Our *K★R 101 Peter/Marie* requires a 7" (18cm) German composition body, and we will use her as an example of stringing a composition body.

Supplies:

GB7 unstrung body
SN1 French Bisque Body Stain
SBR24 Flat Stain Brush
SN50 Nail Stain
SBR10 Detail Brush
Four small washers
Four medium washers
EL7 Elastic
Needle-nose pliers
SCLAMP Stringing clamps
Popsicle sticks

Apply a smooth coat of French Bisque Body Stain to composition body parts using a flat stain brush. An easy-to-assemble drying rack for body parts can be put together with a block of styrofoam and popsicle sticks. Allow all parts to dry well.

To string the legs, tie a knot at the end of the elastic, and thread the elastic through one small and one medium washer. Use needle-nose pliers to push the washers and knot into one lower leg. Thread the proper upper thigh onto the elastic, and continue threading the elastic through the leg hole of the torso and out the neck. Repeat this procedure for the opposite leg. Pull both pieces of elastic taut, and tie a square knot over a popsicle stick.

To string the arms, use elastic and washers the same way as for the legs. Use needle-nose pliers to force the washers and knot into one lower arm. Thread the upper arm onto the elastic, and continue threading the elastic through the arm holes of the torso and through the opposite upper arm. Add washers to the

Stringing GB7 Composition Body for *K★R 101 Marie*

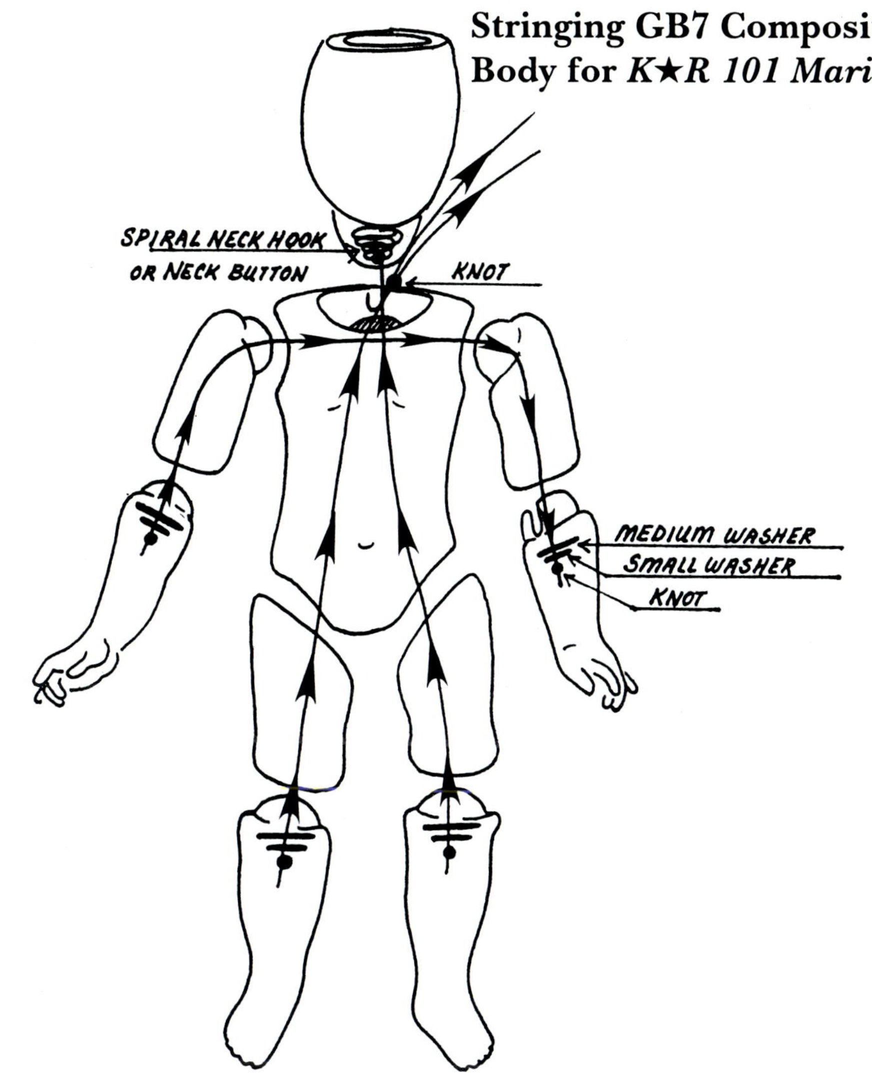

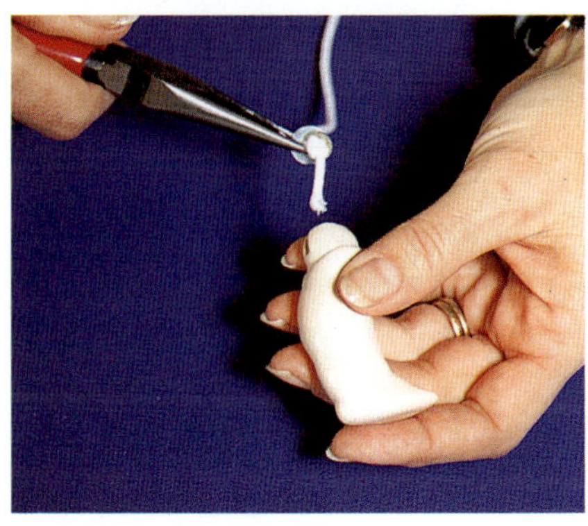

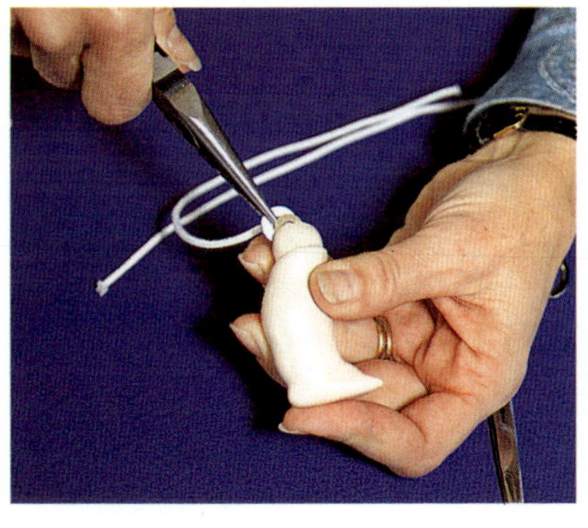

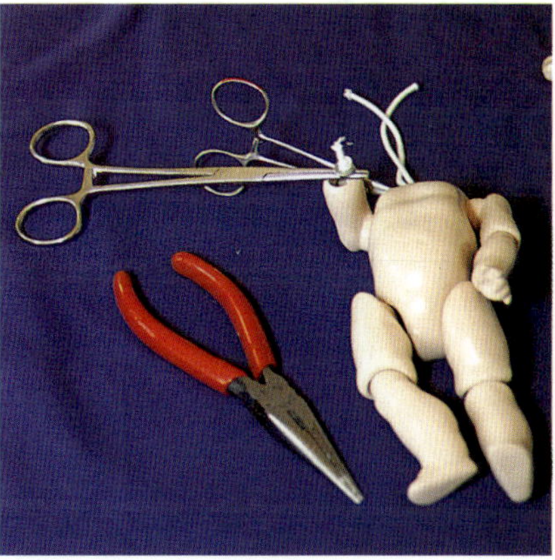

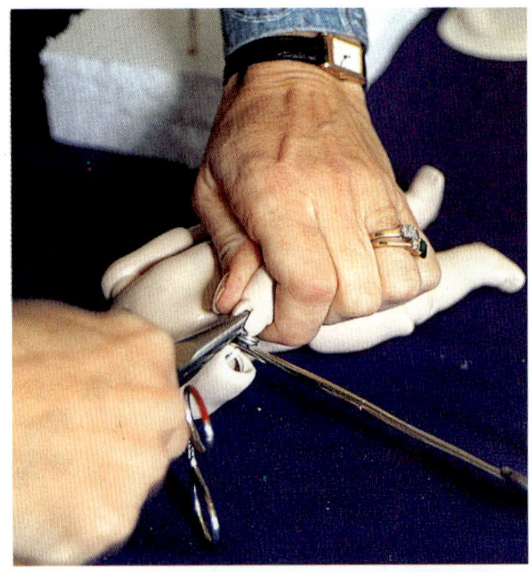

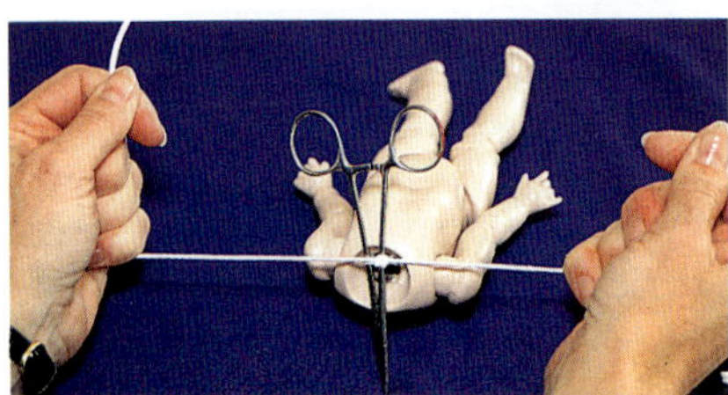

elastic, and pull it taut. Clamp the elastic off with a stringing clamp, and tie a knot up against the washers as close to the stringing clamp as possible. Use needle-nose pliers to force this knot and the two washers into the remaining arm.

Place a neck button or head connector down into the head, and use it to attach the head to the leg elastics.

Optional: Use a Detail Brush and Nail Stain to detail the fingernails at the top of the cuticle.

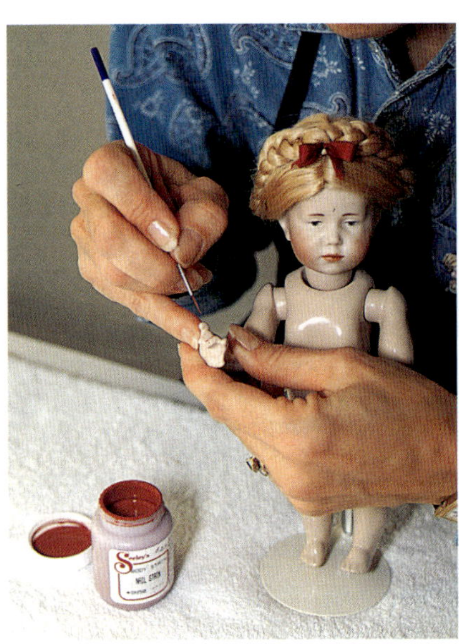

Porcelain Bodies

Some dollmakers prefer all-porcelain bodies for their creations. My personal feelings are that on some contemporary dolls, they are acceptable, but an all-porcelain body is totally unacceptable for a reproduction doll, with the exception of doll-house dolls and all-bisque dolls, 10" (25cm) and under. The major drawback of porcelain bodies is their breakability and their weight.

One of the most irritating things about all-porcelain bodies is the grating sound of porcelain rubbing against porcelain when the doll is moved. This can be avoided by

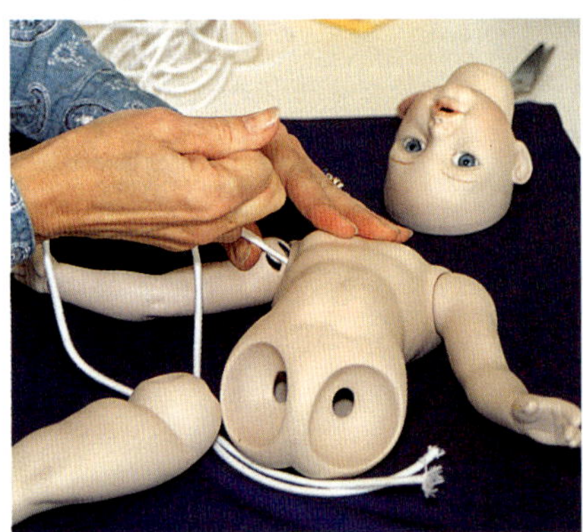

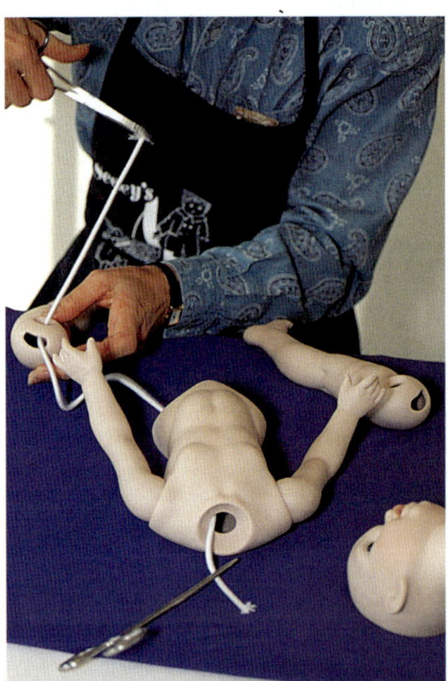

either lining the joints with fine leather or moleskin or painting the joint socket with clear nail polish or varnish.

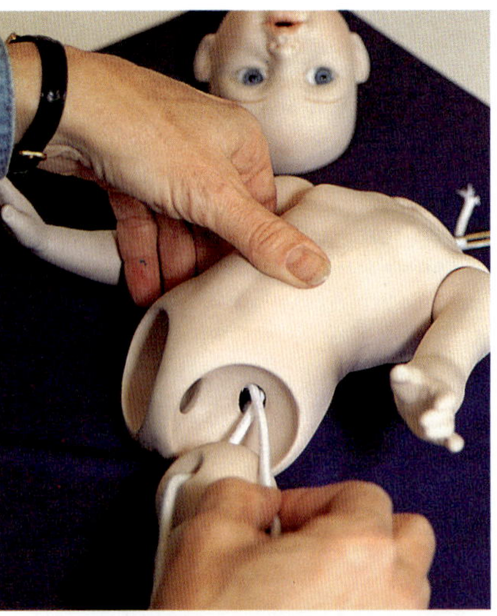

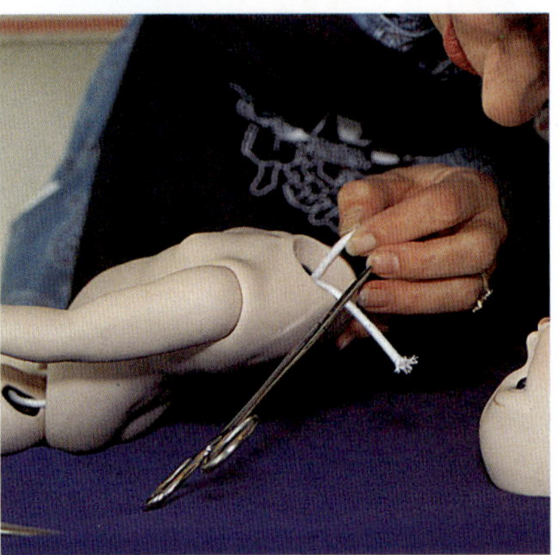

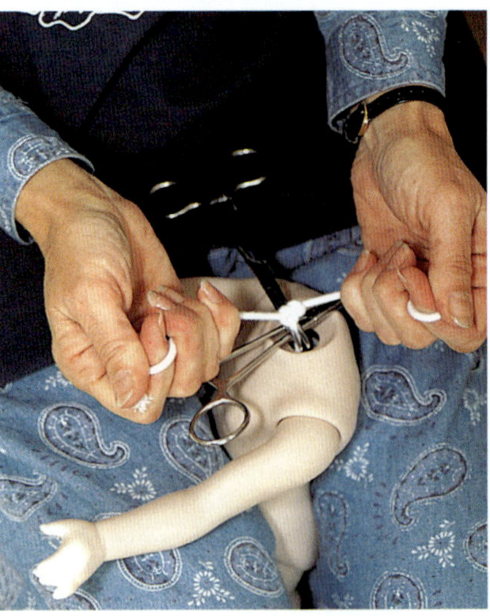

If you like reproduction dolls, consider the all-bisque *Elsbeth, Bluebell,* or *Sweetpea.* There are a number of contemporary dolls with porcelain bodies you will enjoy bringing to life. Choose from the magical fairies *Tanzey* and *Odelle,* available in two sizes, the adorable *Pickles* or

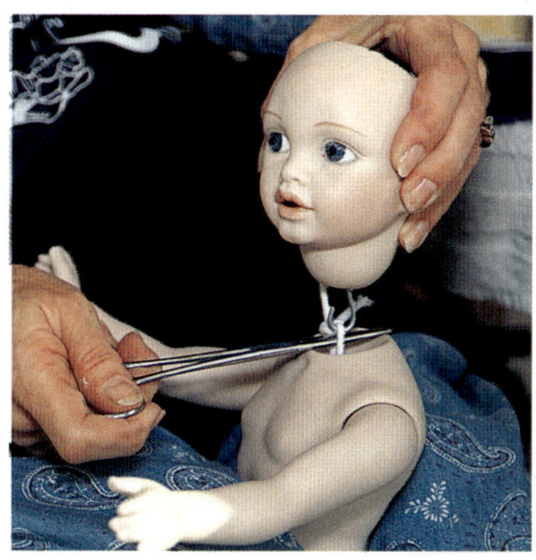

Razen characters, or the serenely-beautiful lady doll *Eve.*

Our lovely *Angel* is put together on a darling all-porcelain toddler body. She is exceptionally easy to string owing to her unique body design.

Supplies necessary to string *Angel:*

- Small circle of soft leather or moleskin
- Clear nail polish
- EL7 Elastic
- Neck button or head connector
- Stringing clamps

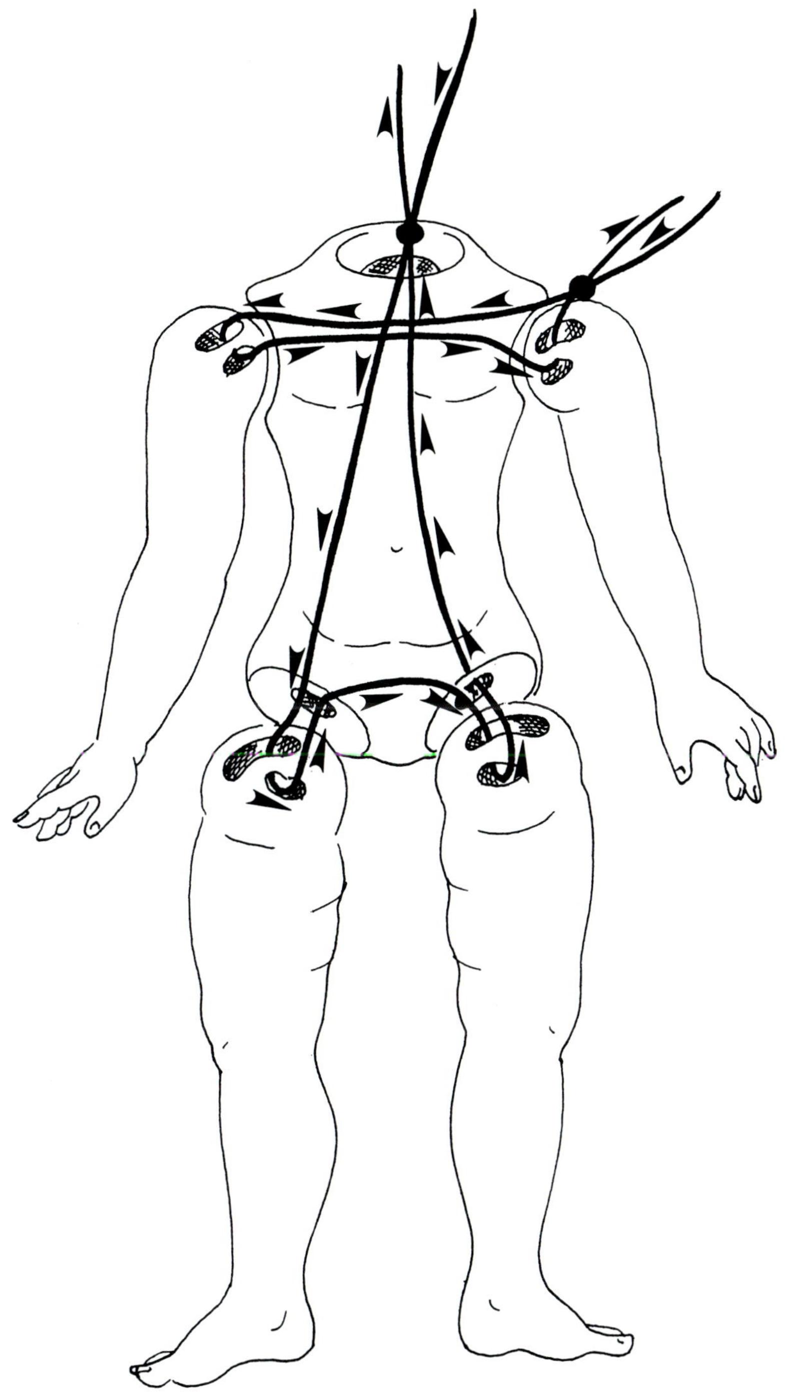

Stringing *Angel*'s Porcelain Body

Baby Chrissy Body

For Seeley mold S872 and A9872 hands.

Materials

½ yard (45.7 cm) tight-weave fabric (trigger, drapery lining, pillow ticking) to match porcelain color
Strong string or nichrome wire for neck and arm casings
Teddy Bear joints: two - 45mm, two - 35mm
Cardboard to cover neck opening
White glue
Small amount polyester fiberfill
Baby Beans™
Thread
Funnel

Note: all seams are ¼" (6.4mm)

Sewing Instructions

Body

1. Stitch darts on body front and body back. Slash darts, and press open.
2. Sew gathering threads along bottom edge of body back.
3. With right sides together, stitch body front to back. Leave 2" (5cm) opening at one neck edge to make sewing bias casing easier.
4. Cut a bias casing 8" x 1" (20 x 2.5 cm), and with right sides of bias strip and body together, stitch around neck edge. Turn bias strip to inside, and stitch in the ditch.
5. Complete stitching of side seam.
6. Insert string or wire in neck casing.

Legs

1. Stay stitch between small dots.
2. With right sides together, stitch toe (point **A** to **B**).
3. With right sides together, stitch two leg pieces around outside edge, leaving an open area for stuffing between small dots. Clip around curved seams. Turn right side out.
4. Repeat for other leg.

Arms

1. Stitch darts. Slash darts, and press open.
2. Stay stitch between small dots.
3. With right sides together, stitch outside edges of arms, from **C** to **D**. Turn up lower arm edge ¼"(6.4mm) twice to form casing. Stitch along first fold. Stitch from **E** to **F**, leaving casing opening free. Clip curves.
4. Repeat for other arm.

Assembly

1. Use 45mm Teddy Bear joints to attach legs to body at large dots.
2. Fill the legs with Baby Beans. Cap off Baby Beans with a bit of polyester fiberfill to hold beans in place, and, hand stitch opening closed.
3. Thread heavy cord through casing of arm. Insert porcelain hand inside arm, thumb toward dart. Pull up cord tightly, fitting it into groove of porcelain. Tie securely. Apply white glue to flange of hand and casing and over knot. When dry, turn arm right side out through opening. Repeat for other arm.
4. Use 35mm Teddy Bear joints to attach arms to body at large dots. Use funnel to fill arms with Baby Beans through opening. Cap off with polyester fiberfill, and hand stitch opening closed.
5. Cut a circle of cardboard to cover doll's head at the neck opening, and glue on with white glue.
6. Fill body with Baby Beans; cap off with polyester fiberfill. **Do not overstuff.** Place head in neck opening, pull string as tightly as possible. Tie off.

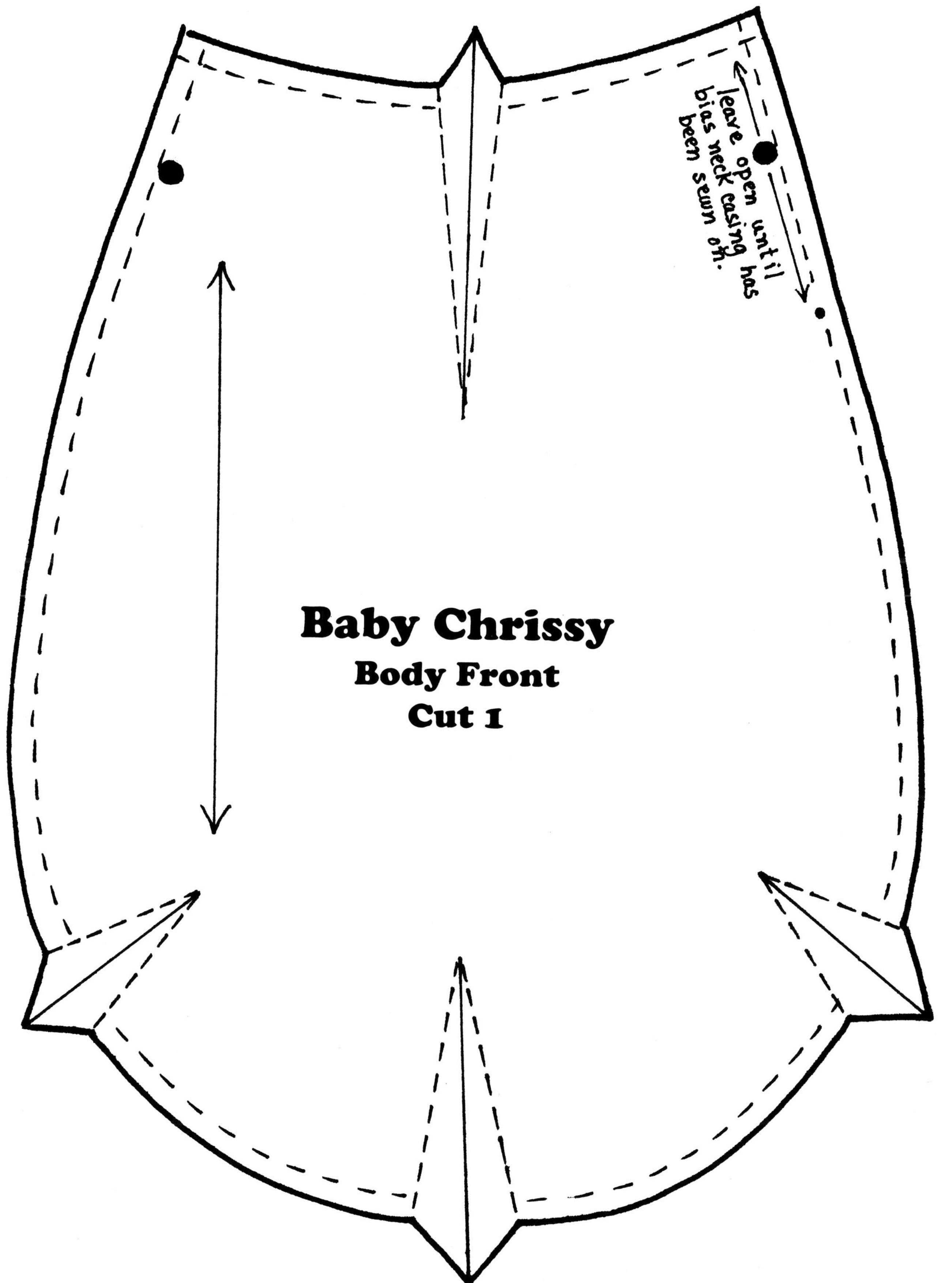
leave open until
bias neck casing has
been sewn on.
Baby Chrissy
Body Front
Cut 1

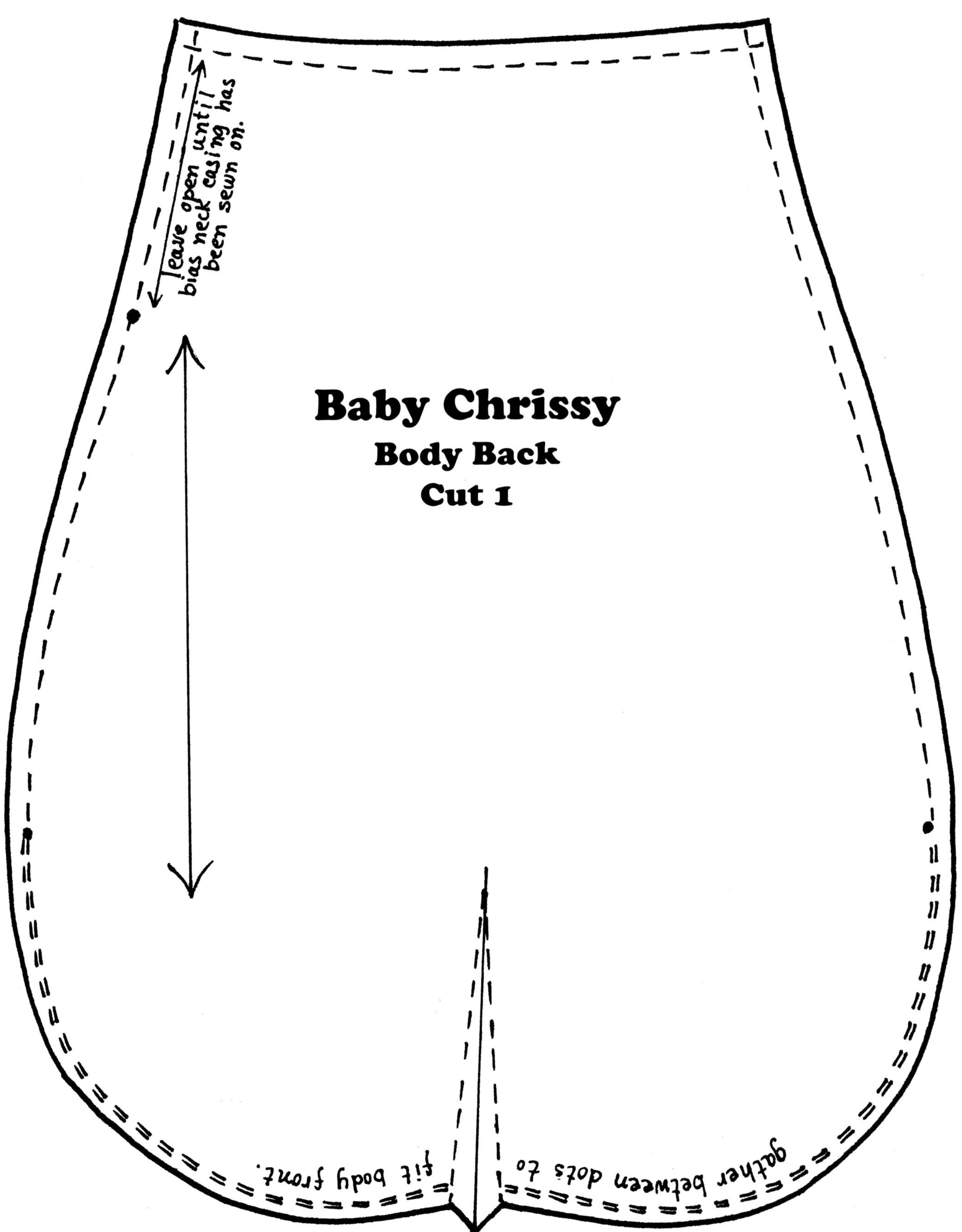
leave open until bias neck casing has been sewn on.
Baby Chrissy
Body Back
Cut 1
gather between dots to fit body front.

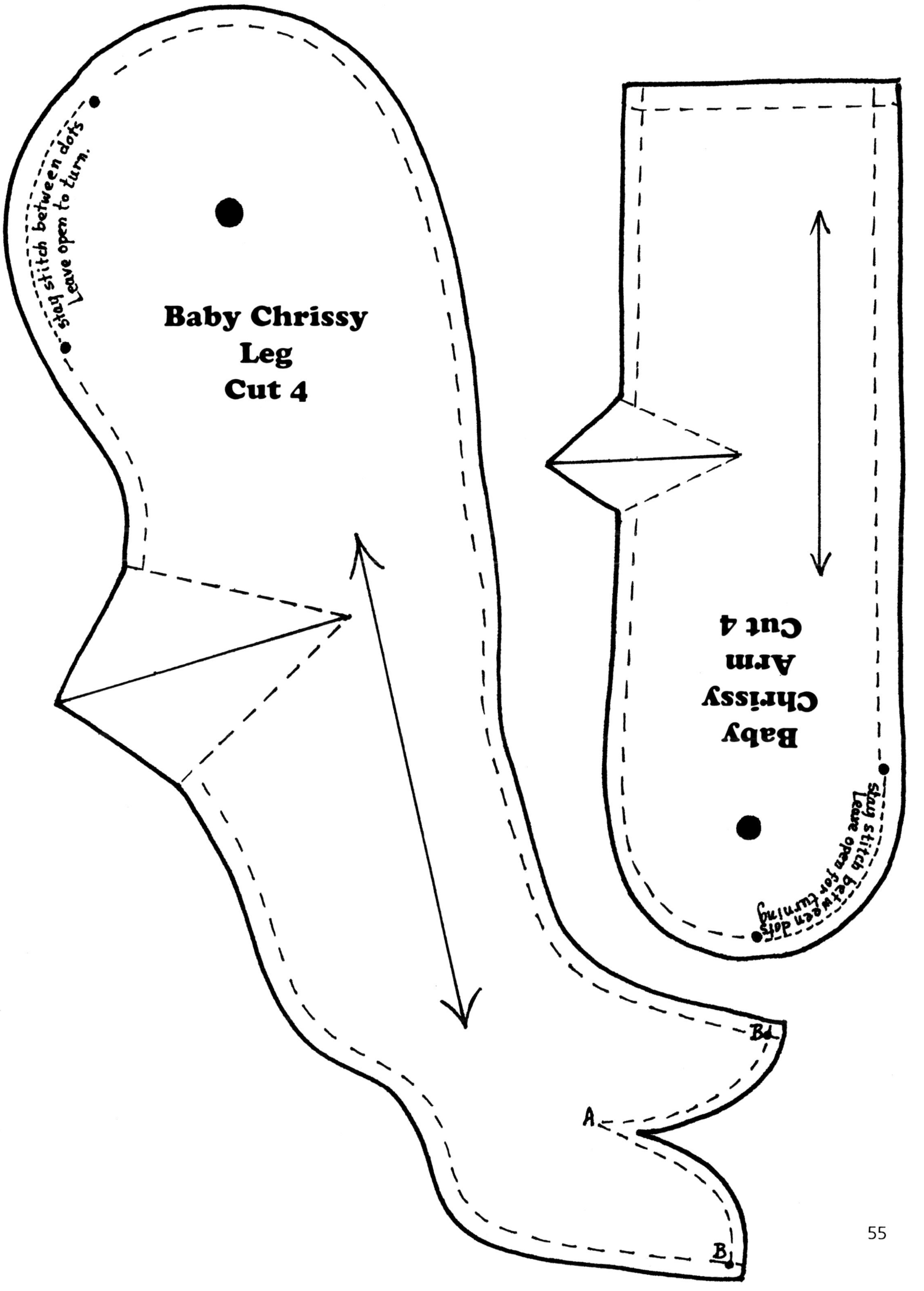

stay stitch between dots
Leave open to turn.
Baby Chrissy
Leg
Cut 4
B
A
B
Baby
Chrissy
Arm
Cut 4
stay stitch between dots
Leave open for turning

11 A Mohair Wig for Marie

MOHAIR IS THE PERFECT CHOICE for a wig to best complement our lovely *K★R101 Marie.* Mohair is the silky, fine, luxurious hair (not wool) of the Angora goat. This hair, after being shorn from the goat, is washed, dyed, and wefted, ready for the dollmaker to create a splendid mohair wig.

Supply List

- Mohair Locks™ in your choice of color
- 5" by 5" (12.7cm x 12.7cm) square piece of matching fabric to make wig cap, or a ready-made Seeley's Wig Cap.
- Thread to match mohair
- Wide-tooth comb
- Wig brush
- Scissors
- Spray bottle for water
- Tissue paper

Step 1.

Begin by purchasing or creating a wig cap from fabric of the same color as the mohair you plan to use.

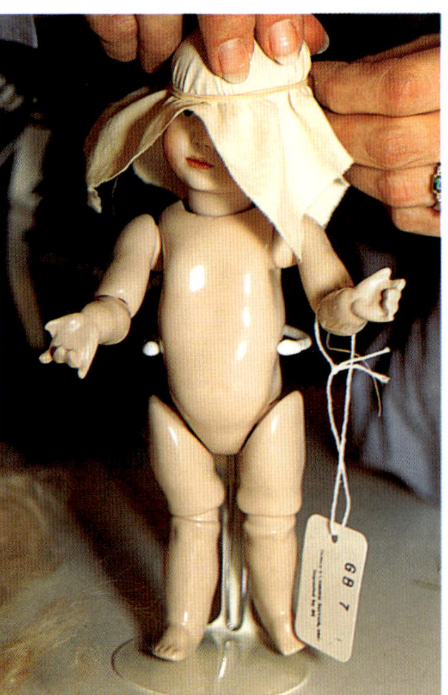

Place the fabric over the doll's head, and hold it in place with a rubber band around the circumference of the head, just above the ears. Make

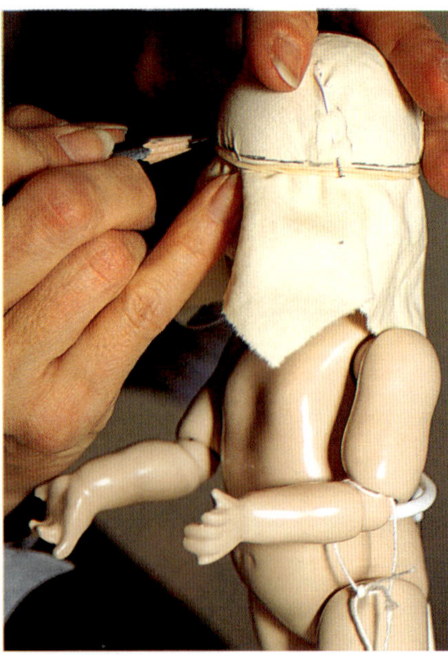

several darts in the fabric, and pin them in place. Mark the center front and center back of the wig cap. Draw a line on the wig cap to mark the center part and also mark the circumference line.

Machine stitch the darts using a small zigzag stitch. Trim the excess material from the darts. Machine stitch around the circumference line twice, using a small, straight stitch. Trim off excess material close to this line of stitching.

If using Seeley's pre-formed Wig Cap, place the cap on the doll's head, and mark center front, center back, and the center part.

Step 2.

Prepare the Mohair Locks by carefully combing out tangles with a wide-tooth metal comb. Use a spray bottle to thoroughly wet the mohair; then, firmly hold the wefted edge, and gently comb though the Mohair Locks to remove any tangles. Allow the mohair to dry.

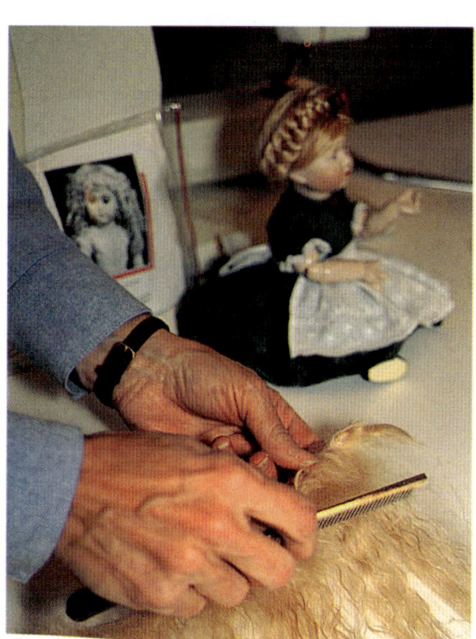

Step 3.

Cut a 7" (18cm) piece of mohair, and use a zigzag stitch to stitch this first row of mohair to the **wrong** side of the wig cap about 1/8" (3.2mm) from the circumference line. Stitch around this first row twice. Turn the wig cap right side out, and place it on the doll's head. Firmly pin the wig cap onto the doll's head.

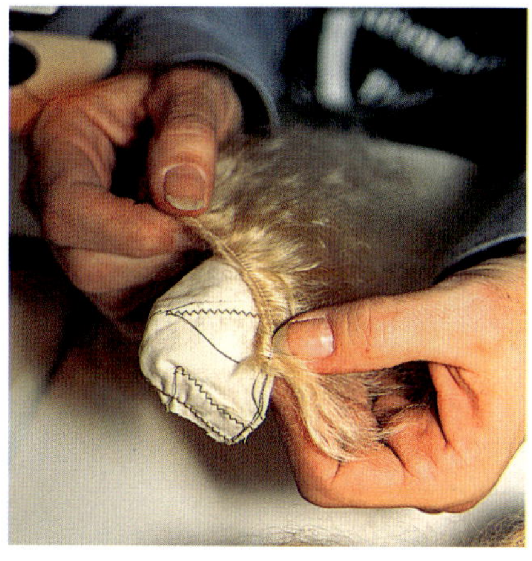

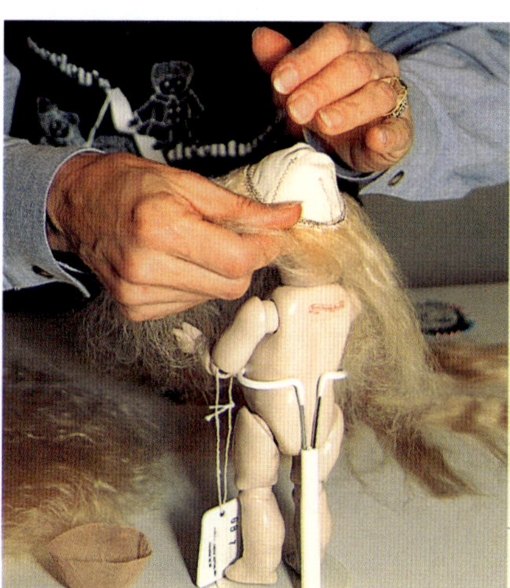

Step 4.

Cut an 8" (20cm) piece of Mohair Locks for the center part. Select the longest and densest mohair for this, and comb it out carefully. Place tissue paper under the wefted edge, and use a small, straight stitch to machine stitch ½" (1.3cm) to the left of the wefted edge. Stitch slowly and carefully so that the mohair is evenly distributed with no gaps. Pull off the tissue paper. Stitch two more rows of straight stitching between the first row of stitching and the wefted edge. Fold this strip in half, wrong side out, with tissue paper between the fold. Carefully

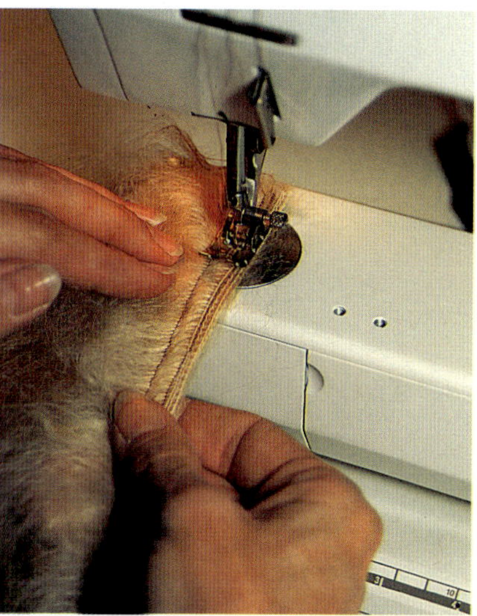

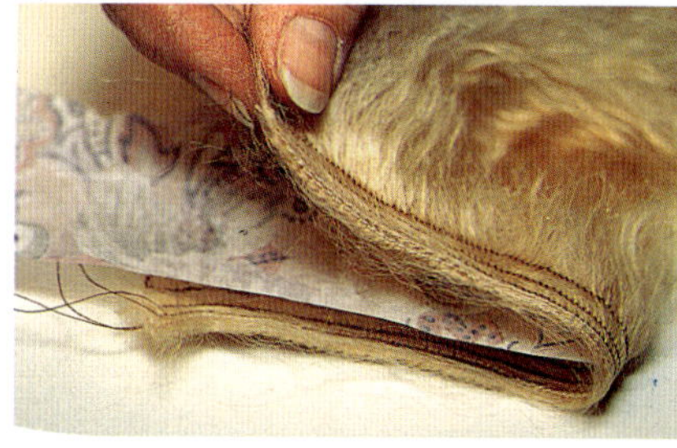

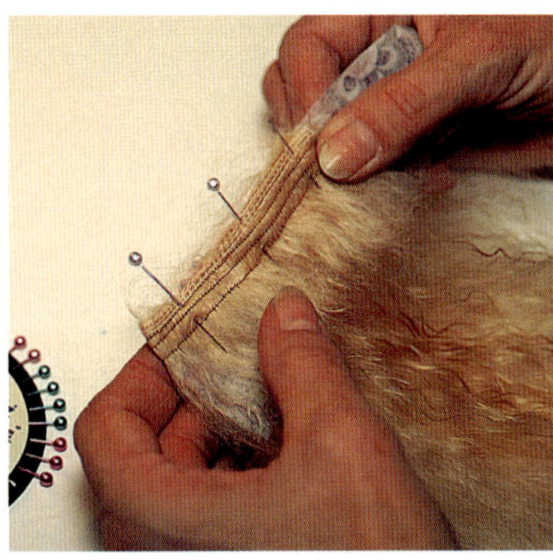

baste the folded mohair together along the innermost row of stitching. Machine stitch along this basting line. Evenly separate the mohair

parting, cover with a damp pressing cloth, and steam press both the

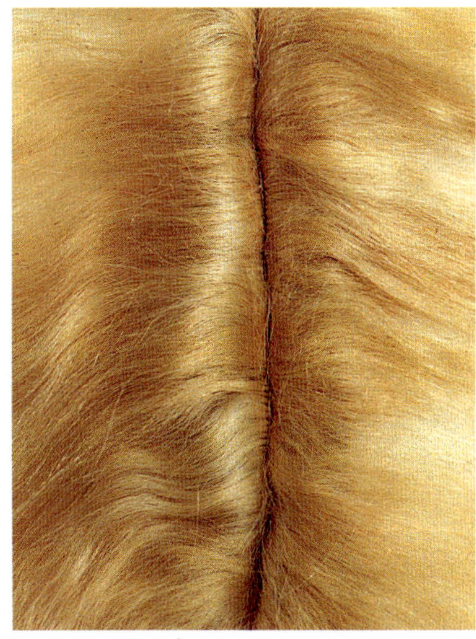

wrong side and the right side of the parting. Remove the tissue paper, and lay this mohair parting aside.

Mohair Wig Stitching Guide for Wig with Center Part

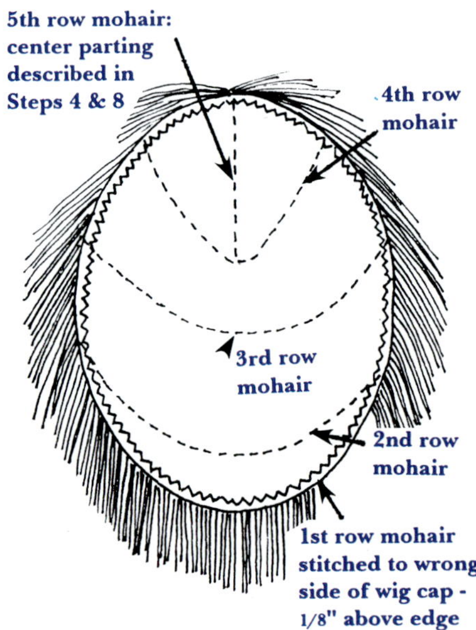

Step 5.

Cut a 3" (7.6cm) piece of mohair, and with the little bits (short ends of sewn, folded mohair) to the wig cap, stitch this piece from ear to ear as on the diagram. Hand stitch this mohair down along the first line of stitching along the circumference of the wig cap.

Step 6.

Cut a 4" (10cm) piece of Mohair Locks, and stitch a second row of mohair ¾" (2cm) above the second row. Stitch this row down along the stitch line for the second row.

Step 7.

Cut a 2½" (6.4cm) piece of mohair, and slipstitch this in a curve ¾" (2cm) above the third row. Stitch this down along the stitch line of the third row.

Step 8.

Place the parting down the center of the wig, pin in place, and stitch it neatly to the wig cap through the center part.

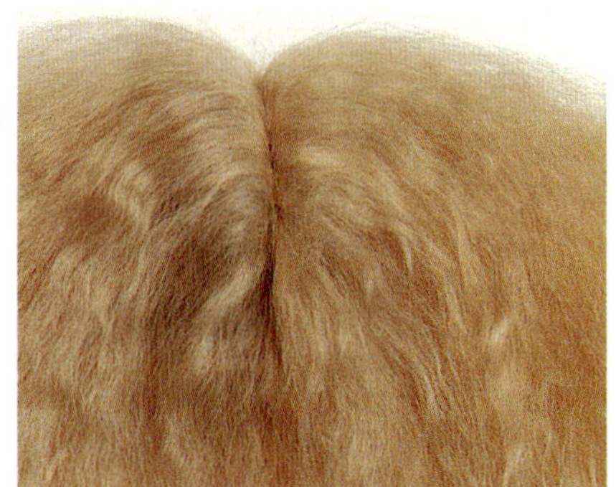

Inside of cap is pencil-marked with sewing lines for mohair rows

Inside of cap after sewing is completed. Note zigzag machine stitching and slip stitching.

Step 9.

Pin the wig firmly to the doll, and wet the mohair with a fine mist of water. Gently comb the hair, and

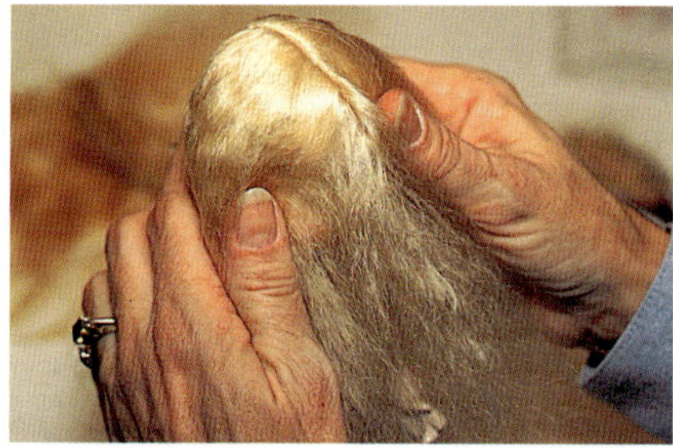

use small rubber bands to fashion a ponytail just below each ear. Braid this hair tightly, and tie it off with thread to match the hair. Repeat this procedure for the other side.

Step 10.

Pull the right braid up over the head, and stitch it in place across the crown of the head. Blend the bits of hair at the bottom of the braid into the hair on the left side of the head. Pull the left braid up over the head, and tuck the bits of hair at the bottom of the braid underneath the first braid. Stitch this braid in place in the same manner as the first.

Other variations are often seen on little *Marie*. Try looping the braids at her ears, and tie them off with pretty ribbons. Leave the braids hanging loosely or tightly coil a braid at each ear.

12 Entering Doll Competitions

"I could never win an award; so why enter?" you say.

Dolls made for competition by Doll Artisan Guild members await the attention of D.A.G. judges.

Why enter? Ask any dollmaker who has entered a Doll Artisan Guild-sponsored competition why they enter, and you'll get answers like "competition is exciting," "competition is fun, and I enjoy the camaraderie of other dollmakers," "I learn so much from the judges' comments," and "My competition dolls are very special to me, and I take more time creating them."

Yes, competition is both fun and exciting. You'll meet many new friends with whom you can share ideas and your love of dollmaking. Competition will bring out your best work. Moreover, the written score sheet you will receive will make you aware of your strong points and your shortcomings and offer suggestions on how you can improve your work. How good are you? You'll never know if you don't take a chance and enter competition.

Many students ask just how their dolls will be judged and what the judges are looking for? In Doll Artisan Guild (D.A.G.) Competitions, dolls are scrutinized in the areas of general overall appearance, workmanship, china painting, wig/painted hair, costuming, and projection of idea. Dolls in **Reproduction Categories** are judged for their similarity to the antique doll. Dolls in **Open Categories** are judged for their creativity and execution of idea. Dolls in **Sculpting Categories** are judged on how well their artistic creativity has been captured in normal human proportion. Most important, **each doll is judged on its**

Each doll is closely scrutinized by the judges. After their careful attention to every detail the judges write their evaluations of the doll's strong points and shortcomings and offer suggestions for improvements to the dollmaker.

own merits. It is not compared with another doll, only an imagined perfect doll. Dolls earning 90 to 100 points receive a blue ribbon; 76 to 89 points, a red ribbon; and 65 to 75 points, a white ribbon. The highest blue ribbon doll in each category receives a "Best-in-Category" rosette. Rosette winners in the Reproduction Categories compete for the top awards, the *Millies,* named for Mildred Seeley. *Millie* awards are presented to the best Professional, best Non-professional, and best Small Doll. The best dolls in the Modern Doll Artists' Dolls Categories compete for the top award of *The Magge,* named for Magge Head Kane. *Eva's Choice* award is given to the doll of Eva Oscarsson's choice in Imagination Dolls Categories. Rosette winners in Sculpting Categories compete for the *Rolf Ericson Award for Outstanding Doll Sculpture.* Top awards may only be won one time. If a top-award winner from a previous competition is chosen to receive a top-award again, it will receive a Special Honorary *Gold Rosette.*

Your chance of winning a ribbon is very good especially if you have taken D.A.G. seminars.

Dolls are entered anonymously, and the judges are knowledgeable, unbiased, professional dollmakers with expertise in the many areas of dollmaking. The entrant is assured a concerned, constructive evaluation aimed at helping him/her become a better dollmaker. Score sheets are given to each entrant upon reclaiming his/her doll.

Doll Artisan Guild-sponsored competitions are held worldwide. Listen to the excited buzz in the competition room. These are the sounds of happy, enthusiastic dollmakers, bent on improving their skills. Resolve now to enter a doll in the next D.A.G. competition, and join this group of dollmakers, who have learned to get the most possible out of their dollmaking hobby.

GLOSSARY

All-Bisque Dolls - Dolls made completely of porcelain bisque.

Antique Doll - Generally refers to a doll created before circa 1930.

Applied Ears - Ears molded separately from the head and applied to the head after it has been removed from the mold.

Artist Doll - Original doll created by contemporary artist circa 1930.

Articulated - Jointed with one or more joints; as in articulated doll body.

Artisan - A skilled crafts person.

Authentic Reproduction - Doll re-created from a mold with a genuine resemblance to the original.

Automatic Shut-off - Mechanical device that shuts off kiln at desired temperature. Usually refers to Kiln Sitter.

Automaton, Automata - Mechanical doll(s) usually on a base with movable arms and head. Concealed mechanism is key wound and often connected to a music box.

Baby Beans™ - Plastic pellets used in contemporary baby bodies to give weight and make them more positionable.

Ball-jointed - A doll with separate balls in the joints for articulation.

Bébé - French term for doll depicting a young child.

Bevel, Beveling - In dollmaking, the act of rounding out the eye sockets inside the head.

Bent-limb Body - Usually applies to five-piece baby body with slightly-bent but not jointed limbs.

Bisque - Unglazed fired porcelain with matt surface.

Bisque Doll - Doll with bisque head. Body material may vary.

Blanket Prop - Porcelain prop compressed into sheets. *See* Porcelain Prop.

Blush - In dollmaking, it generally refers to rosy color subtly blended onto cheeks, knees, elbows, etc.

Blush Pac™ - Pre-mixed cheek blush packaged in a snap-lock container.

Bonnet Doll - Doll with molded bonnet or hat.

Breather - Doll with nostrils pierced through the bisque.

Brush Traveler™ - Convenient case for storing and transporting brushes.

Casting - The act of filling a mold with slip; also refers to the molded shape.

Character Doll - Doll sculpted to resemble a real child in contrast to the "dolly-face" doll. Example: *K★R 101 Marie.*

China - Glazed porcelain with shiny surface. Also china doll.

China Doll - Early doll with shoulder head and limbs of china. Circa 1840s through 1880s.

China Paint - Overglaze colors which, when mixed with the proper medium, are used for painting on top of a glazed or bisque surface.

Circumference, Circ., C. - The measurement around the widest part of the doll's head. Example: 10-inch head requires a size 10 or slightly larger wig.

Clean-up Tool - Tool used to remove seamlines from greenware or soft bisque.

Closed Mouth - Mouth not cut open.

Composition, Compo, - General term for doll body material, including papier mache and wood pulp.

Cone - Cone-shaped or bar-shaped ceramic material used in the kiln to measure the amount of heat received by objects during the firing process.

Cone Supports - Metal supports which, with the actuating rod, hold the junior cone in the kiln sitter.

Contemporary Doll - Dolls created by living artists.

Crow-quill Pen - Pen with thin-tip nib used with china paint to paint eyelashes and eyebrows on dollhouse dolls.

Deflocculant - Chemical additive to slip that is necessary to cause clay particles to remain in suspension.

Doll Artisan - Certified Doll Artisan title given to D.A.G. members who have completed Apprentice courses, I, II, III.

Doll Sponge - Fine grain sponges used for application of overall wash.

Dolly-face Doll - Doll with idealized child features.

Dome Head - Round head, usually with molded or painted hair. Crown is not cut out.

Draining - The act of removing excess slip from the mold.

Dust-free Technique - Method for cleaning soft-fired ware in a wet state, which eliminates all greenware dust.

Elements - Coils of heat resistant wire which convert electrical energy to heat in the kiln.

Ethnic Dolls - Dolls representing people of various races or nationalities. Example: Indian, Black, Oriental dolls.

Eva's Choice - Doll Artisan Guild top award named for Eva Oscarsson, given to best imagination doll.

Eye Sizers - Tools used to bevel eye sockets in greenware or soft bisque heads.

Fan Brush - Fan-shaped brush made of bristles used for painting hair to simulate texture.

Fashion Doll - Doll dressed as adult or older child, usually on a shapely body. Also called Lady Doll.

Featherknife - Scalpel-like tool used to cut out eyes and crown.

Fettling - Removing seamlines from greenware or soft-bisque.

Filbert Blender Brush - Full, oval brush used to blend color.

Finger Tool - Fine, saw-like tool used to separate fingers.

Firebrick - Refractory bricks used to insulate firing chamber of kiln.

Firing - The heating process used for maturing greenware and to fuse china paint or glaze onto the bisque.

Firing Cone - The desired cone for the ware being fired.

Firing Sand - Pure, smooth, ball-bearing-like grains of sand used on the kiln shelf to facilitate movement of ware during firing.

Flange Neck - Neck with rim at edge for holding it onto cloth body. Usually for the baby dolls.

Flirty Eyes - Eyes that move from side to side and also open and close.

Flux - A white powder that can be added to china paint to help it bond to the bisque or to add gloss to the paint. Also helps the paint to move freely.

Glaze - Ceramic paint applied to greenware or bisque to give it a glass-like surface when fired to maturity.

Glaze Brush - A soft bristle brush used to apply glaze.

Gold Rosette - Award given to a top-award winner who has previously won a top award. The *Millie,* the *Magge, Eva's Choice,* and *Rolf Ericson's Award* may only be won once.

Googly Doll - A doll with large glass or painted eyes, looking to the side.

Greenware - An unfired clay object.

Guard Cone - Witness cone, one cone hotter than the Firing Cone. Guard cone should remain nearly straight after a good firing.

Guide Cone - Witness cone, one cone cooler than Firing Cone.

Half Doll - Dolls with bisque torso and upper arms, made to attach to a cloth lower body; often used for pincushions, tea cozies, powder boxes, and other items.

Head-torso Doll - Head and torso are one piece.

Hesitation Lines - Rings formed on casting during pouring when rate of pouring slows or stops.

High-fire Firing - Firing to a high temperature; cone 2 and hotter.

Hydrated Alumina - A white powder used on kiln shelf to allow porcelain to move (shrink) without warping during the bisque firing.

Incising - The act of carving into greenware or soft-bisque; usually name and date.

Intaglio Eyes - Painted eyes with the pupil and part of the iris recessed.

Kaolin - A very white clay used in formulating porcelain slip.

Kiln - Heating chamber made of firebrick, used to fire clay objects and glazes to maturity.

Kiln Furniture - Posts and shelves used in kilns to take full advantage of the firing space.

Kiln Sitter, Sitter - Mechanical device for shutting off the kiln to the desired temperature with the use of a Junior cone.

Kiln Wash - Protective material, brushed onto the shelves of a kiln. Used as a separator to keep objects from adhering to the shelf.

Kiln Vent -Device that safely removes fumes from kiln during firing.

Lady Doll - *See* Fashion Doll.

Layette - Wardrobe for baby doll.

Leatherhard - Term that refers to greenware, still damp. Ware that holds its shape but is not dry.

Liner - A fine, long-haired brush, used mainly for fine lines.

Luster - An overglaze used over a fired glaze for an iridescent effect.

***Magge,* The,** Doll Artisan Guild top award named for Magge Head Kane, given to best modern doll artist's doll.

Marotte - Decorated doll head on spindle. Makes music or sound when twirled.

Matting Agent, Matter - White powdery substance added to china paint to reduce shine.

Maturity - The point in firing at which the bisque becomes fully vitrified.

Mechanical Doll - *See* Automaton.

Medium, Media - Liquid(s) used to mix with and dilute china paints.

Mildew - Phenomena occurring on underfired bisque after china firing. It manifests itself as a myriad of tiny black specks.

***Millie,* The** - Doll Artisan Guild top award in dollmaking, named after Mildred Seeley.

Milette - Small French dolls in the Seeley line with leather, bisque, or composition bodies no taller than 8".

Mohair - Hair from the angora goat often used for doll wigs.

Mohair Locks™ - Wefted mohair.

Mold - The hollow plaster form into which slip is poured in order to form various doll parts.

Mold Keys - Concave and convex indentations and protrusions which serve to match mold halves and hold mold together for banding.

Mold Soap - Liquid used for lubricating models and molds in mold making. Residue sometimes found in new mold.

Molded Hair - A dome-head with hair detail sculpted on the head.

Neck Button - Button, usually wood, with a hook attached for fastening a doll head to the body.

Neck Joint - Where neck and shoulders separate.

Nichrome Wire - Wire with resistance to high temperatures. Can be used to stilt ware during china fire, for neck hooks, and to make springs for wobble tongues, etc.

Nodder - All-bisque doll with jointed neck only.

Oil-Base Technique - Using oil-base media for china painting.

Opaque - Not translucent.

Open-closed Mouth - A doll mouth that looks open, sometimes with teeth, but with no opening into the head cavity.

Open Mouth - Mouth that has been cut open into head cavity.

Optivisor™ - Magnifying lens for close-up painting worn on head like a visor.

Original Doll - A finished doll created by the sculptor.

Overall Wash - Flesh-tone tinting of bisque surface. Usually the first china-paint firing.

Overfired - Fired to temperature above maturity. Results in shiny, blistered, and pitted ware. Color has fired out.

Overglaze - A low-fired material used over a fixed glaze or on a vitreous surface such as porcelain. China paints are overglaze colors.

Palette Knife - A small flexible knife used to grind, mix, and condition paint on a tile.

Paperweight Eyes - Glass eyes that have a dome over the iris. Usually in French dolls.

Papier-mâché - Paper-based material used to make dolls and bodies.

Parian - Fine, white, untinted bisque. Also Parian doll.

Parian Doll - Doll made of Parian without overall wash. Most often shoulder-head doll with molded hair.

Parisienne - French Lady doll.

Pate - Dome-shaped cover for doll heads with cut-off crown. Used to round out head.

Peep Hole - Opening(s) on the sides of a kiln for observing progress of firing and for venting.

Peep Hole Plug - Cone of refractory material used to close the peep hole.

Pierced Ears - Ears with holes for earrings - sometimes cut into the lobe, sometimes into the head.

Plasticizer - Substance mixed with porcelain slip to turn it into porcelain clay.

Porcelain - A combination of clays fired to high temperatures. Vitreous and usually translucent.

Porcelain Doll - Doll with at least its head made of china or bisque.

Porcelain Prop - A fibrous material used to support greenware during the firing. Must be handled with caution.

Portrait Doll - Doll sculpted to portray a particular person. Example: the George Washington doll.

Post - Item used in kiln to support the shelves.

Poupée - French term for doll depicting a lady.

Pourhole- Mold opening through which slip is poured and drained.

Prop - *See* Porcelain Prop.

Pyrometer - An instrument that measures the temperature and the progress of a firing inside a kiln.

Regional Costume - Doll clothes representing costume worn in a particular region.

Replica - *See* Reproduction Doll

Reproduction Doll - A doll made from a mold taken from an antique doll and presented as close as possible to the original.

Rolf Ericson Award - Doll Artisan Guild top award for original doll sculpture.

Rouging - Applying red or pink color on cheeks or body.

Self-supporting Cone - Witness cone with built-in base, requiring no cone holder for support.

Seam, Seamline - Raised line on casting where mold halves meet.

Screwgles™ - Spiral neck hooks used for easy attachment of heads; especially those with closed crowns.

Separators - Materials such as high-fire kiln wash and hydrated alumina which prevent two pieces of porcelain from adhering to each other during firing.

Shadow Brow - Light brow shape often applied and fired on before individual feathered eyebrows are painted.

Shoulder Head - Doll's head and shoulders in one unit.

Shoulder Plate - Doll's shoulders, separate from the head.

Silica Sand - *See* Firing Sand

Sitter - *See* Kiln Sitter

Sleep Eyes - Eyes attached to weight which causes them to close when doll is laid down.

Slip - Liquid clay.

Slip Whiz™ - Slip mixer with top adapted to fit Seeley gallon slip container.

Socket Head - *See* Swivel Head

Sodium Silicate - Used for deflocculating slip.

Soft Firing - Soft-bisque firing (cone 018 to 019 in kiln sitter) for preparing ware for dustfree cleaning.

Soft-Fired Ware - Partially bisque-fired ware, ready to be cleaned with the Dust-free Technique.

Spare - The section of a cast piece that is usually cut off and discarded.

Square Shader - Flat brush with straight-edge used to apply large areas of paint, to blend color, and for other decorating techniques.

Stilt - High-fire metal support used to hold up glazed pieces.

Stringing - Assembling all-bisque or composition doll bodies with elastic.

Stringing Clamp - Forceps-like tool used in stringing doll bodies.

Stylus - Tool used to carve detail and incise name and date in greenware and soft-bisque.

Swivel Head - Head that turns on a shoulder plate or composition body. Also called Socket Head.

Test Cone - Clay form used for checking kiln temperature. *See* Cone.

Thermocouple - Temperature-sensing part of the pyrometer.

Thermal Shock - The result of sudden change of temperature inside kiln during cooling. Often results in hairline cracks and shattering.

Tint, Tinting - Applying a wash or light coat of color to bisque.

Translucent - Something that allows light to pass through, such as porcelain.

Transparent - Something that can be seen through, such as glass.

Underfired - An object fired to a temperature not high enough to properly mature the clay body. Pieces appear chalky and have a porous feeling and immature color.

Vitreous, Vitrified - Non-porous, waterproof; changed into glass-like substance.

Warpage - Distortion of shape by rough handling after casting or by uneven heating and shrinking during firing process.

Waterbase Technique - Using waterbase media for china painting.

Wet-Cleaning - Technique for cleaning soft-fired ware without creating dust, mainly called Dust-free Technique.

Wet Scrubber - Thin abrasive pad used for wet cleaning of soft bisque.

Witness Cone - Cone used to monitor a firing. Usually set of three. *See* Guide Cone, Firing Cone, Guard Cone.

Wobbly, Wobble Tongue - A tongue made from plaster, composition, porcelain, or fimo, cemented onto a spring that enables it to move.

About the Author

HELEN SCHAEFFER is a Master Dollmaker, Instructor, Researcher, Author, Doll Promoter, and Business Woman. In addition, she possesses the invaluable advantage of deep insight into advanced techniques in both low-fire and high-fire ceramics, insight gained during many years as a ceramic artist and instructor before porcelain dollmaking took over her life.

I have known Helen for many years and have admired her drive to perfect everything she touches, be it the firing of porcelain or the attention to an individual student. When the challenge of writing a complete, state-of-the-art book on porcelain dollmaking for the beginning and intermediate dollmaker came up, Helen Schaeffer was my first and only choice. The result, *Beautiful Dolls Made Easy,* bears witness that my instinct was right.

Helen's earlier books, *The Joys of Porcelain* and *Oriental Ceramics,* established her as a leading authority on porcelain and its decorating techniques. In addition, for many years, she has been a leading contributor of technical articles in *Popular Ceramics, Ceramic Arts & Crafts, Doll Crafter* and *The Doll Artisan.*

Helen lives with her husband, Stan, in Bernville, Pennsylvania, where she operates her successful business called Plum Creek Dollmakers, researches dollmaking techniques, advises Seeley's on new product development, and enriches the dollmaking world with continuous articles on all aspects of porcelain.

Rolf Ericson

Word processing and proofreading meticulously executed by Barbara Seneschal.

Design, layout and page production by Jean Manley.

Editing by Maureen Dugan.

The dolls enjoyed a day's outing at WOOD BULL ANTIQUES, Milford, N.Y., with photographer Lilly Smith.